BRIGHTER
REALMS

PATH

MEDIA

pathmediapublishing@gmail.com

ISBN: 979-8-9853857-0-0 (paperback)
ISBN: 979-8-9853857-1-7 (ebook)
ISBN: 979-8-9853857-2-4 (hardcover)

Library of Congress Control Number: 2023924564

Ordering Information:
Special discounts are available on quantity purchases by corporations, associations, and others. For details, contact pathmediapublishing@gmail.com

Publisher's Cataloging-in-Publication Data:
Names: Daniel, Stephen, author.
Title: Brighter Realms: Awakening Awareness of Your Higher Self / Stephen Daniel.
Description: Los Angeles : Path Media, 2024. | Also available in ebook and audiobook formats.
Identifiers: LCCN 2023924564 (print) | ISBN 979-8-9853857-0-0 (paperback)
Subjects: LCSH: Self-help. | Self-consciousness (Awareness) | Mind and body. | Philosophy.
   | Healing. | BISAC: MIND, BODY & SPIRIT / General. | SELF-HELP / General.
Classification: LCC BF151 .D36 2024 (print) | LCC BF151 (ebook) | DDC 153--dc23.

BRIGHTER
REALMS

AWAKENING AWARENESS
OF YOUR HIGHER SELF

STEPHEN DANIEL

PATH
MEDIA

To the nonphysical systems and to my mentor, whose unwavering support helped me create Brighter Realms for humanity.

And to my Earth-bound partner for her vision and love.

CONTENTS

INTRODUCTION

Our lives begin with the first awareness of ourselves. The first time we saw our reflection in a mirror. The first time we rode a bicycle. The first time we felt love. The first time we found a purpose and contributed to the world—filled us with the awareness of our independence and freedom of spirit. We are at the frontier of awakening our awareness of everything and everyone, including what's yet to be discovered. With every gut feeling, every impulse, and every thought, we look beyond ourselves, furthering our awareness of who, what, and why we are. We awaken our potential to experience greater fulfillment, happiness, and peace. The adventure is only limited by the boundaries we create and the lens we focus. Along my path, I began investigating what makes our existence possible. Where do we come from and where do we go from here? Like many people, I felt I was a part of something much bigger than myself, that reality was far more than could be seen or touched. I started taking stock of out-of-body experiences and visions I had been aware of since childhood. To help me understand memories, I opened a dialogue with a voice that had always been present in the back of my mind—what I call my higher self. The relationship I developed led me to write *Brighter Realms*. The result is a book that offers the potential to experience a deeper connection to wholeness. Wholeness means unity with our higher self, where insight, intuition, and creativity flow. I say "offers the potential" because each person's experience is different. Some people have read the book and discovered a distinct awareness of their higher self. Others felt the book gave them fresh insights into the nature of existence. Therefore, it's more accurate to say the book offers the possibility to experience a deeper connection to wholeness. Yet I have also observed people who are unconsciously tuned into their higher self, benefiting from expanded awareness and peacefulness. However, there is no one-size-fits-all technique I can offer readers. Everyone's relationship with their higher self is as unique as their fingerprint. The higher self has a different approach to its human counterparts and agreement is specific to each person. The main goal of the book is to bring awareness to the vast intelligence of a higher self each of us has in common. *Brighter Realms* represents a fundamental reality long forgotten by humanity, examining other worlds where my stories originate, written as a reminder of your inherent abilities to benefit from the extensive resources available to you. In the greatest sense, you are already there, able to tune into insight, intuition, and creativity as an instinctive awareness of the larger reality at play. That is your birthright. You are the connective tissue to independence and freedom of spirit which knows no boundaries. There's a saying that the body knows what the mind has forgotten. The body holds the memories from our past and the awareness to live in the present. I expanded this idea in another context: Our true body is the energy we are, our essence. Everything else—intellect, ego, emotions, and physical body—are parts of the suit we wear. As an essence, we are an extension of our higher self with existing links to other worlds. Our greatest fulfillment comes from living with purpose guided by the enormous resources available when we tune into our essence, offering us the capacity to access our higher self. We may not be aware of our essence, and that's fine, because it functions with or without our knowledge to immerse us fully in the life experience. We may think our essence is a part of us, when in actuality our essence *is* us. We can learn to heal old wounds, live in our purpose, and find deeper fulfillment when we grow and stretch our evolution with our essence leading the way.

PROLOGUE

As a child, my mother flew in her father's airplane, searching the clouds for angels. The little girl with large, curious eyes explored the world around her to understand life's meaning. When she was uncertain about finding angels, her father suggested she look inside herself. He was teaching her to look at the world with discernment. They shared a strong bond. In her early 30s, she was grief-stricken and inconsolable when he died of a sudden illness. For many months she woke up with tears and went to bed heartbroken until she heard his voice one morning. She lifted her head from her pillow and saw him standing at the foot of her bed. He told her he was happy and wanted her to be happy. He asked her to let him go. A powerful feeling of calm came over her. She realized her father was not far away.

When her mother died years later and we were driving home from the funeral, she told me she could feel her presence close by. My mother had transformed her grief by discovering existing connections to worlds beyond and was no longer separated from the bonds to her parents.

Before my mother passed away, I shared these thoughts with her. She replied, "You have the story right—I'm not sure about worlds beyond." While she acknowledged the wonders and mysteries of life, she also believed in proof and validation. What she accepted or rejected about reality had little bearing on the unconscious forces, which formed her outlook. When her father's voice came that morning, she listened. But she started feeling better because she was determined to resolve her grief without consciously understanding the process that got her there. She proved she could make the leap and find inner peace.

I've met many people who have shared stories of transcending boundaries and experiencing otherworldly events they could not place in the context of the physical world. Some lost loved ones. Some had accidents. Others recalled insightful dreams or moments of intuition, revealing clues to their larger role in existence. Most agreed they glimpsed spiritual realms and experienced reality beyond the physical world. They unconsciously understood their essence as their core self already interfacing with other worlds. They may live in different corners of the Earth, yet they share a common ground of understanding. Specifically, they are no longer separate from other worlds but are unified with them and the clarity they bestow. The discovery has expanded their outlook, giving them independence and freedom of spirit.

The bridge to worlds beyond is never lost, although it can be forgotten. Many of the problems in the world can be better understood by unifying with the spiritual worlds all people have in common. Our separation from these worlds has led us to societal divisions and fragmentation, breaking down connection to the fundamental reality that unifies us with our energetic system—an intelligent, organized association of interrelated relationships acting as the family from our origin before birth.

Imagine if we humans were observed by a race of beings from a distant planet. They would see us as a source of inspiration with an immense creative drive, a boundless sense of adventure, and vast spiritual resources. They would also see a separation from the knowledge of who and what we are as if each of us is a single individual adrift on a raft in the middle of a vast, empty ocean. They could suggest we unify with other worlds and each other in this one.

The vibrant inner life of children expresses the worlds from which they come. The instinct to sustain these links supports mental and psychological well-being. Just as the physical world inspires artists, the instinct to explore beyond ourselves is a powerful motivating force, producing profound artistic representations. Music, sculpture, and drawing are a few artistic expressions that put us in touch with our essence as a link to worlds beyond. Access, however, is not just reserved for the artistic. Parents play with their children and experience a subtle interface with other realms. Some people walk to become quiet inside or lie down for a nap to unhook themselves from the external world. Others take a more determined approach by meditating.

There's no mystery here—taking the path to other worlds is what people do in ordinary day-to-day life to experience peacefulness and intuition from their nonphysical origin, sharpening instincts, and providing adaptation in the physical world. Reaching beyond ourselves is as natural as picking up an object with our bare hands to study its detail or opening a book to benefit from its knowledge. The only specific action required to go from here to there is a desire to yield to our essence— the part of us we can't see in a mirror, our fundamental self that can only be experienced. As I write these pages, gaze at a sunset, laugh with my partner, or feel my mother close by, I am engaging my essence to connect with other worlds in everyday interactions.

The countless ways people move beyond themselves is an innate characteristic of human nature. We already participate in a much larger story, wherein encounters with brighter realms is an unfolding theme in our lives. All share the capacity to transcend the dense boundaries of mere physical existence and experience the broader meaning of worlds beyond.

Of course, having the desire for a greater understanding of

ourselves sets the stage for our personal evolution, moving us closer to wholeness. The journey to brighter realms beckons us to explore what more there is to existence, to reach beyond ourselves to the Larger Field where our stories shine in the wonder of our existence. The stories in this book are not based on conceptual beliefs, such as ideologies, religions, dogmas, or the paranormal. Nor is this work a study of mythologies. In this book, beliefs are fundamentally inconsequential to the understanding people have in common—for example, knowing or feeling that loved ones who have died are not far away. Knowing or feeling we are more than our bodies. Knowing or feeling there is far more to reality than meets the eye.

Yet beliefs are an interminable thing that can creep into just about every idea or thought. I have done my best to put my beliefs aside and tell my stories from a purely experiential point of view as I explore the spiritual worlds I have been learning about since birth. For the writing of this book, I describe spiritual worlds as the worlds we come from before birth, where we reside when not in physicality, and to which we will return someday. I use terms like "nonphysical" or "Larger Field" to describe the entirety of spiritual worlds—what are essentially limitless environments within infinite worlds to which everything known and unknown happens and where human beings have the potential to interact by way of their essence.

I use the term "higher self" to describe what is infinitely more massive than a human being's essence. I think of the essence as a temporary energetic extension of the higher self, and its presence in the physical world is a person who eventually returns home to their higher self. People also have associations of interrelated relationships representing their energetic family in nonphysical environments. That's right—we have a physical family and we also have an energetic family, and our higher self is a part of that family. But an individual's system is much more—a very large number of related higher selves, each with one or more human extensions in physicality, and there are countless systems in the nonphysical. All these terms can just as easily be interpreted in the realm of belief. The terms help illustrate the ideas I introduce. I challenge readers to suspend their beliefs as I introduce concepts about humankind's origin, where insight, intuition, and creativity originate.

The challenge is getting ourselves out of the way by learning to recognize our essence as our fundamental connection to the larger reality at play.

Brighter Realms is my collection of stories about unity and wholeness, echoing humankind's desire to explore its deepest existential questions of why they exist. Consider the ideas presented here and make up your own mind. I invite you to step across the threshold into worlds beyond us, where essence unifies with higher self, creating synchronicity in brighter realms.

ONE

The Barber Chair: Seeing Beyond Ourselves

One of my earliest memories occurred when I was five years old in the barbershop where my mother took my brother and me once a month for early morning haircuts. The barber chairs stretched the entire length of the shop like time machines in a windowless corridor. Each shiny red vinyl chair was surrounded by empty space, making them look like island stations facing tall mirrors, producing so many reflections it was hard to tell which chairs were real and which were echoes. With each step I took, the shop turned darker—except for the chair where my barber waited. A single light bulb on the ceiling made that chair look larger than the others.

As I climbed into the seat, the barber moved levers to lift the chair until my head fit neatly in the palms of his hands. That's when I first saw it. Hanging on the wall between two mirrors was a large painting with a gray sky and billowing clouds filled with angelic light. What grabbed me was an object in the middle of the painting. It was a man dressed in medieval clothing, his coat flapping wildly in the wind as he fell through the sky with terrifying momentum.

Staring at the painting, I struggled to place the man in the context of his world. His solitary plunge made me feel troubled, sparking my imagination and igniting an obsession. He was falling backward, facing the direction from which he was falling. He didn't appear to flail his arms or legs or attempt to turn himself to face the direction he was falling. It was his expression that made me especially nervous. As I peered closer, his face was strangely peaceful—even pacified and content—as if he didn't know or care he was falling. I couldn't stop thinking he would keep falling until he hit the Earth below. Except he was so high up in the sky, maybe there *was* no Earth, no ground, nothing to stop his fall. I imagined he would keep falling in the sky forever. The painting intensely captivated me every time I went for my haircut.

I couldn't begin to understand the emotional currents rushing in the stream of my thoughts, the sensations sparring inside me, utterly unrestrained by my inexperience—the uncertainty of the man's predicament. His acceptance of the place he was in. Would he hit the ground and die? Did he know where he was? Was he going someplace? Or was he coming from someplace? Did he care? Did it matter? Powerful feelings carried me to the edge of the painting's strange world as reality forced questions I had no way to answer. I wondered if I would lose my grip and fall into the painting and *become* that man. As inexplicable as my struggle felt, it lessened when another feeling rose inside me. It caused a nearly opposite reaction and had the peculiar effect of tempering the uncertainty I felt. In the presence of the painting I would experience a freeing effect, as if I too was letting go and falling eternally through the sky without the weight of earthly constraints.

I was moved by the sense of adventure the painting instilled in me. The powerful presence of my emotions is what links this memory to me. All these years later, the long row of barber chairs, the emptiness of the shop, and the bowl-like haircuts my brother and I received are only a small facet of the memory, inadvertently attached to the larger significance of the painting's impact on me. To my five-year-old self, the feelings inspired by the artist's vision stirred a deep unconscious awareness of my essence, moving me across a bridge from the physical to the nonphysical realm.

If I stared long enough at the painting, I would feel off balance and lightheaded as if I was standing at the edge of the physical universe looking into another, into a view with no end. Then a shift occurred—a sense of wondrous freedom descended and encompassed me. Physical boundaries dissolved. I found myself in an expanse of endless space. I could see a part of myself looking back at my physical self. Then I could look the other way at other selves, other aspects of me in nonphysical worlds, and be as if in all places at the same time. Lighter feelings washed over and comforted me with a profound recognition I was not alone. I perceived my existence in that infinite realm. I went with it. I let it unite me with the part of myself that occupies other worlds. A part of me was unaware of what was taking place—but to another part of me, the views and sensations made perfect sense. I was reestablishing an integral part of who and what I am—a unified wholeness innately connected to the Larger Field.

The painting offered my first insights into the larger reality at play. The artist cleverly provided an otherworldly perspective, setting the stage to facilitate existing links to the worlds beyond and, thus, enabling me as the viewer to invite forward what was already present. A well-executed painting is like an invitation to a common ground where worlds behind the physical world can be experienced. This is what art can do. I was unconsciously carried by an artist's thematic underpinnings to become momentarily unified with the Larger Field. From that location, I could experience the full breadth and impact intended by the painting. There are a great many artists operating from other world perspectives who set the stage for viewers to be transported to worlds beyond.

Today, I can gather my memories of the barbershop with the awareness of my essence. At my young age I was shown previews of another reality without being conscious of its role in my life. As my young self was making sense of the painting's deeper meaning, I was learning about the bridge to the Larger Field, which is always close by. Years later I realized that the artist and I were on a parallel path, except I was missing what the artist had: experience. To my older self, the artist's vision showed me a pathway from here to there by making it possible to glance into his or her inner domain, helping me recognize my own inner domain. The lighter feelings showering me. The calm inner peace. The view with no end. The warm feelings lifted, carried, and enabled the painting to open a pathway beyond me. As naturally as breathing air, an invitation was dispatched to rendezvous with my higher self and energetic system. They are always there, awaiting the opportunity to come forward. In perspective, it was actually me—my essence—tuning in to do what is likely the most natural capability all possess—to interact with our energetic counterparts.

The experience set into motion my first insights revealing who I am, what I am, and where I come from. These first glimpses could easily be interpreted by psychologists as a child's active imagination. I have often found the interpretative nature of psychology to offer interesting parallels to other worlds beyond. It's ironic that to discover worlds beyond ourselves we must explore the worlds within us. The idea that people possess a vast mental, psychological, and spiritual landscape is widely accepted in the modern world. However, these explanations attempt to interpret the internal landscapes through the lens of psychology without the benefit of investigating the essence.

The framing of psychological concepts is a natural response to the needs of society attempting to make sense of the unseen and unknown dimensions of human beings.

My personal journey to learning about my essence came slowly. In my youth I was too preoccupied by life to inquire about such matters, even though like all people my essence was at the forefront of the unobserved reality happening inside me. I was mostly unaware of its behind-the-scenes role to keep me grounded with my higher self and energetic system.

As the years progressed, I continued to have transcendental experiences, giving me a view of a larger reality through small windows that seemed to contradict everything I was taught. It's no wonder—physical life took 99 percent of my attention, leaving only a fraction of my awareness on the fleeting curiosities of other worlds that were inviting me in. Once I began exploring, other worlds entered the orbit of my thoughts. As I shared my stories with people, I was uncertain how to interpret them. I could sense a significant purpose to my essence as if it was already a player in a larger reality, and yet my intellect and ego had little understanding of what it all meant. It seems my physical self was inadequately prepared to keep up with the awareness of my essence.

The turning point came in my teens and early 20s when I started to look closer at my transcendental experiences. With desire and effort, I began to encounter my essence and things began to shift. I discovered the essence operates in 100 percent of reality and the physical self represents a small yet significant facet of that reality. There's no way to calculate physical perception versus the awareness of essence. The true scope of existence can only be experienced. In its core message, *Brighter Realms* is the journey to the larger reality at play. Human beings are at a crucial juncture in their evolution. We are turning a corner into a fantastic new world of understanding. This material suggests human connections to nonphysical environments do exist and will one day be universally accepted.

I share a lot of memories throughout the book. One or two of them take place when I am in my first year of life. I don't remember my birth and I can only imagine my feelings in the early years of motherly embrace. But I do have many vivid memories—as unusual as it may seem—about specific events that took place through my early years and beyond. I have an extraordinary gift to remember details. But memories are still fragments and, in my case, packed with emotions and seared into my being by the good fortune of recall. I used to believe the abuse I experienced by my biological father shocked memories into my being.

While it is uncommon for people to remember their early years, I am one of the fortunate who does remember. The recollection of events shaping my life has often amazed my family. I have impressed them with my ability to remember minute details from dreams, and other experiences during my childhood. I have faint memories of the small home we lived in when I was about three. It had a leaking roof, wet floors, and a clothesline stretching across the yard. I don't remember my mother's worry that we didn't have enough money or the year my father started delivering babies and our lives got better, but I remember sliding a chair next to a kitchen counter at around age four. I climbed up and stood where I could reach a high cabinet to pull little bottles out with my small hands until my mother found me, screamed, and made me tell her if I had eaten any pills. With tears in her eyes, she took the bottles and flushed them down the toilet. It is just the fragments, but sometimes more, that stay with me, perhaps embraced by my essence to be recalled in memory.

As I gather my experiences from my current life perspective, I recognize a broader view. To be born in the physical world is to inherit existing connections to nonphysical worlds, which account for the vast record of spiritual experiences and storied mythologies passed down through the ages since the beginning of human civilization. My moments with the barbershop painting taught me that people interact unconsciously with nonphysical environments, and interface with their energetic counterparts, empowering the potential for synchronicity and unique perspectives from the most primary observations of our relationships here and beyond. I also learned about my essence—the part of me enabling connectivity to insight and intuition from my higher self and energetic system. Another perspective I gained has to do with the soul. Spiritual traditions have taught that humans are made up of two parts, a physical body and an immortal aspect, which is given names such as the spirit or soul. I prefer the term higher self to describe the energetic origin of a person. I think of my essence as the most tangible aspect of my being—who I am beyond my body, intellect, ego, and emotions, operating as the vital link to my higher self in the Larger Field. I have been a student of the nonphysical for 30 years, yet I am a newcomer to self-exploration and discovering my capabilities. I have transcendental experiences like many people, and I'm still learning about what they mean to me. Our otherworldly experiences can place us firmly in the driver's seat of self-discovery. But to learn about ourselves—to truly grasp a deeper understanding of who we are—begins with awakening awareness of our higher self. No one knows us better.

TWO

The Discovery of Essence: Our Dreams Can Take Us Home

I was about four years old when I was handed a small magnet and shown how to pass it through the sandbox at my kindergarten school—I was captivated by the tiny slivers of metal clinging to an invisible field. Perhaps this first encounter with unseen forces aroused an unconscious awareness that there was more to reality than meets the eyes.

Hand-in-hand with my mother, we would walk down the street from our house and cross the busy boulevard. Once safely across she'd set me free to walk to my kindergarten school. Taking myself down the sidewalk, up a little ramp, and into the classroom was my first act of freedom, giving me a sense of independence from others, yet connecting me to them. Every day in kindergarten I was asked to lie down for a class nap even though I wasn't tired. But the teacher insisted a nap was good for us. I usually stayed awake, but sometimes I slipped into a dream-filled state far away from my classmates. Upon waking, I hardly knew where I was. After a moment my life came into focus and it all made sense. I had been asleep. These first recollections gave me the distinct feeling I had been someplace else, in another world and back again.

The events of my early life led me to explore the natural world as a steppingstone to the infinitely larger reality. At home, I shared a bathroom with my brother and sisters, with two sinks and two medicine cabinets facing each other on opposite walls. I opened one mirror slightly, gazing into the other mirror, and saw many reflections of myself stretching into the distance. I imagined entering the mirror to join myself in another world. Known as the infinity mirror effect, a small fraction of light bounces off the mirrors casting the illusion of multiple reflections. This phenomenon sparked my curiosity that there was more to myself than could be seen in a reflection.

One warm cloudy day while exploring my backyard, I came across a palm tree that stood a little taller than me. I noticed two palm leaves sandwiched together. My curiosity grew when a few red-winged, black-spotted ladybugs crawled around the edges of the leaves. I used my small hands to separate the leaves. That's when I saw hundreds of ladybugs living between them. Many appeared asleep, some moved slowly, and others were very animated as if searching for something. When I showed my mother, she suggested I let a ladybug climb onto my hand

and make a wish. "When a ladybug opens its wings and flies away," she said, "your wish will come true."

Over the coming days, I made many wishes and watched many ladybugs unfurl their wings and take to the sky. I wished for my father to come to dinner. My mother had kicked him out of the house, but I wished they would get along.

One day I went to the palm tree and the ladybugs were gone. They had disappeared as if they had never been and left me wondering when my wishes would come true.

Years later I'd always offer my hand to a ladybug and make a wish, even though I knew ladybug wishes were made for a child's imagination. I cherish the memory of my mother's optimism. She knew wishes were the first rehearsal of our dreams, endowing us with the capacity to manifest.

In my early 40s I was going through difficult changes. My biological father passed away and left me feeling unrequited in our relationship. In my work life, I was writing and pitching screenplays to production companies. Things were moving slowly, and I was feeling pent-up and unsure about my future. I stood on a balcony at the edge of the canyon where I lived. A ladybug appeared on the railing. I placed my hand close so she could climb on. I wished to find my way through my difficulties and emerge fulfilled and happy. Upon that wish wings unfurled and the ladybug took flight.

A split second later a bird swooped by and swallowed the ladybug in its beak. My heart skipped a beat. This was serious,

I thought. My wish had been killed and with it my dreams. A moment later I broke out in laughter, mostly at the seriousness with which I made my wish and watched it be eaten by a bird. I said to myself, "This is the way life is. Dreams don't always come true, but the hope they inspire fills us with meaning and purpose."

For months after that day, a part of me did not live down the loss of that ladybug. The season changed and a warm day came when I had another ladybug encounter. As usual I placed my hand close to her and she climbed on. I repeated the wish I had made without any reluctance. The ladybug unfurled her wings and I watched until she became a tiny dot against the sky. The beautiful red-winged, black-spotted insect filled me with hope and joy. It was a playful moment that was unexpected and transformational. On the wings of a ladybug my mood was lifted and my purpose reignited.

Indeed, wishes and dreams are the rehearsal of our thoughts to confer with worlds beyond ourselves and put into motion life's push onward and upward. These experiences revealed a bridge to my encounters with brighter realms.

Another nature-inspired encounter took place one spring morning when I again walked hand in hand with my mother on the sidewalk to a friend's house. I left her side and headed down the driveway. She watched as I turned a corner out of her view. In front of me, a garden spread out with flowers and trees in bloom. That's when I saw it—a butterfly gliding straight toward me. Then another butterfly with the same red and black colors followed in its path. I watched the two winged creatures fly circles over the garden, captivated in the wake of their flight.

A peaceful feeling washed over me. I felt indistinguishable from the living things around me like there was no separation— we were made of the same stuff. The colors were incredibly vivid and bright. At this moment a soft voice in the back of my mind said, "This is who you are." I was filled with a wondrous sensation of being whole. I had discovered interconnections with all things living. But I could not stay long in the extraordinary place. After a moment, I was back in my life having stepped through a door into the playfulness of the universe. I felt in those few seconds I had glimpsed where I came from. I was too young to understand the full meaning of the experience, but not too young to see the clarity in front of me. Today, I am keenly aware of the path I took, merging me with my original home in worlds beyond. These experiences were among my first teachers encouraging further self-exploration and discovery.

To suggest my experiences with the ladybugs and butterflies were simply the unfolding of my imagination is inaccurate. Children arrive in the physical world to experience life. Development depends on testing the limits and boundaries of their worlds. Yet the worlds children come from play an equal role in development. To observe a child at play is to witness them instinctually interacting with worlds beyond.

Other worlds are also available to adults. However, it

takes a childlike openness to look beyond the dense physical boundaries. Beyond the apparent limits of physicality exists a fundamental reality that can't be seen, touched, or measured.

My transcendental experiences showed me I was reaching beyond the physical world. The significance of my essence was spreading awareness, expanding my view in all directions, and revealing the bigger picture of my existence. I was also learning that physicality has enormous intrinsic value yet narrows the possibilities of experience if allowed to become the sole point of focus. Our essence is the springboard to the Larger Field from which we originate.

Our Dreams Can Take Us Home

People are like trains. You can see the engine in front, the body, intellect, ego, behaviors, and personality. But you can't see what fills the tracks behind that, the essence of a human being. Our essence is arguably the most human part of us supplying the connective tissue to the wealth of resources from our nonphysical family. Yet our essence is hardly human at all. If we strip away our physical self, what remains is essentially energy. As an essence, we are connected to our system and the many interrelated members of our energetic family. Our energetic counterparts represent the extraordinary denominator all human beings have in common.

At birth we are introduced to the physical world. As life takes over, the demands of civilization overwhelm us with the need for conformity. As we mature, our parents and teachers introduce structure and discipline, creating new forms of tension and conflict. Growing up means becoming relevant to the world we find ourselves in. By early adulthood, the relentless push to join life can outweigh even the powerful instincts to sustain our rich connections beyond us. Our once-thriving inner lives become diminished, lessening the connectivity to the wealth of unified wholeness with our counterparts. As we become adept at focusing on the values we perceive are important in the physical world, we can lose sight of the bigger picture that our dreams and happiness come from inside us.

Tuning in is what children do naturally as they are closer to the worlds they come from, born with the innate familiarity to interact with the playfulness of nonphysical environments. They know no other way to exist but to reflect their essence in everyday interactions. Children begin life without the limits imposed by societal and cultural influences. They have not yet absorbed the physical world and its many distractions, and they naturally access internal resources to adapt and thrive. They possess powerful instincts to maintain connectivity to their origin, where they access their nonphysical energetic family's remarkable organization and intelligence.

About 20 years ago I visited my brother's home and talked with my nephew. He explained he was four years old and had lived in his house since he was born. I asked, "Do you remember where you were before you were born?" He stared at me for a long moment—his expression turned pensive as he searched his memory. He gave my question meaningful thought and then asked humbly. "Do you know where I was?"

He took my breath away and made me smile. In response to my question, he hit the physical boundary he could not see past. My nephew had no memory of where he resided before birth. Yet his question showed a keen interest in looking beyond himself, reflecting a deeper introspection beyond the mere few years of his life. By his manner, I observed him trying to riddle out his past and comprehend his existence beyond his present. In response, I told him he came from other worlds like everyone. "You have forgotten them," I said, "Someday, you'll remember."

I think every human being asks similar questions during his or her lifetime. The question of where we come from and where we go from here is the first step to discovering our wholeness. Watching my nephews and nieces grow up, I often observed them engage their surroundings with the vibrancy of an active inner life, the closeness of spiritual worlds instilling them with stunning directness, presence, and clarity. At times they demonstrated remarkable knowledge and wit, as if born with an understanding of subjects from other times and places. They may not have remembered their energetic origin, yet they unconsciously acted with access to inner resources in an ever-present communication between worlds.

As children, the worlds we come from provide a wealth of

resources, including the capacity to show caring and love. Our benevolent values are reciprocated by our parents and others with whom we share life's journey. But the core of benevolent values comes with us from the nonphysical and instills our essence with the humanity we recognize among one another. We humans are born with the capacity to give and receive love inherited from our nonphysical family. These qualities represent a fundamental knowing to act with love informed by wholeness. Life gives us the stage to develop our emotional capacity and express what already exists within us.

For most people, transcendental connection occurs without conscious participation or awareness, for the fundamental human capability is the potential to link to worlds beyond and be informed by them. Humans are born with links to nonphysical environments just as they are born with links to the physical world. Crossing between worlds fosters connections in both realms, giving rise to the independence and freedom to transcend boundaries and discover purpose in all worlds.

Since childhood I have felt a part of something much bigger than the world around me, like another world was taking place inside me. I wondered if other people knew about the nonphysical worlds that were rich in colors and extraordinary light. My experiences aroused my thoughts and provoked my imagination, beckoning me to understand what more there was to life than I could see or touch. When it came to writing this book, I needed a starting point.

For this reason, I chose to explore feelings in the unfolding drama that makes life so fantastic. To feel is to live. To feel is to remember. Feelings link the past to the present and reveal broader insights into who we are. In my youth I wasn't tuned into my feelings, yet I was unusually sensitive to them. I was discovering my memories were primarily made of feelings originating in physical and nonphysical worlds. For years I wasn't able to voice or recognize my feelings. I kept them hidden from myself. If I experienced anxiety, sadness, or happiness, I veiled them behind a shy, quiet personality where they remained my best-kept secrets.

My inner, repressed feelings unconsciously caused me to distance myself from people and life itself. But I never stopped feeling. I had no choice. I am the way I am, although I eventually reached the age where I began to make sense of feelings and their emotional origins. I learned to take stock by journaling extensively. I searched for places inside me I had not been and opened myself to new experiences and ideas. My investigation showed me how feelings could be a link to our energetic origin. In the balance between paying attention and tuning in we can learn to listen to our essence, which is already well-connected to our system and beyond. As a child I was relieved to learn people had otherworldly experiences as I did. I vividly recall an animated television commercial featuring a woman sleeping in bed. Fantastic swirling colors surrounded her in a dream world. She began to rise out of bed and float in the room. The colorful wonderous patterns expanded. Soon the bedroom walls dissolved and she took flight. The sequence was narrated by a soothing female voice saying, "Have you ever fallen asleep and dreamed you are flying? If you have dreams like this, you are not alone."

My flying dreams made me feel I was different from other people. The commercial assured me I was not. Sometimes I would fly at great heights over trees, mountains, or oceans, brimming with wonder in my exploration of worlds where the colors were far more intense and vivid than anything in my physical life.

I often found myself in places that had no resemblance to the physical world. I would merge with fields of color and light which were as aware of me as I was of them. Instantly, I might shift locations from a tree-filled landscape to an ocean or a room with light that came out of nowhere, moving in and out of multiple environments in the blink of an eye, showing me who I was through the places I had been. The overwhelming sense of familiarity filled my awareness with, "Oh, yeah, this is what I'm about."

When I traveled to other environments, I often had no memory of myself as a boy named Stephen, living with my family in a house, as if I had forgotten that part of me and moved on to places where I existed without the need for my physical identity. The feeling of my existence was not defined by the places I was passing through. Rather, the places I traveled were a part of me. I woke up in the morning feeling as if days or years had passed. Then memories of my life filled me with a rush of excitement. I was relieved to be in my bed, in the place and time where I left off the night before. I thought to myself, "I know where I am. I'm in my bedroom, in the house where I live with my family." I always felt a sense of missing the places I came from, as if returning to my bed took me away from the brighter realms. I felt a little sad I couldn't stay longer but I was also happy to be back in my life.

Often I entered other environments with the full recognition of my body waiting for me in my bedroom. These lucid dreams made me aware of other worlds I could enter with the ease of opening a door, and they were as tangible as the world I had come from. Or I would wake up half asleep, drifting between worlds and wanting with all my will to stay in the dream world. I liked returning at my leisure. I enjoyed leaving my physical life behind, as if I existed solely in brighter realms and the physical world was merely a place to visit. Sometimes I returned to my bedroom as if I had no choice. My desire to stay in other realms was overridden by something bigger than myself, what I've come to understand was my higher self guiding the process. It was pointless to argue. Other times I could stay longer. Never long enough, it seemed.

For years I did not talk about my dreams with people. The first time I saw the TV commercial of the animated person, I knew there were people like me. The commercial ended with the letters "TM" for transcendental meditation. In the 1960s the TM movement was in full swing. They were trying to get the word out that people could learn to transcend the physical world and experience spiritual worlds. Over the years I would see the TM commercial and marvel at the animated character leaving her body and flying into other realms.

Around 1970 the TM commercial stopped running. The commercial inspired my first insights into the subject of nonphysical environments and was instrumental in forming beliefs I would examine in later years. The animated person made it look easy to bypass the limits imposed by the physical body, as if taking a casual stroll in other environments was a regular occurrence. Knowing other people had similar experiences was comforting.

During my teens and early 20s I continued to be an inadvertent explorer of the transcendental. At that time, however, I was preoccupied with figuring out the usual things teens and young adults deal with. Yet my experiences in other realms made me feel connected and at times unsure. I began unhooking from my body regularly and leaving my bedroom, floating around the rooms of my home. Occasionally, I panicked when I realized I was away from my body. In my rush to get back, I'd pass through walls and doors and hit my body with a jarring force as if the Earth was shaking. Other times I found myself floating over the sidewalk outside my house. I would rise into the sky and fly over the city, at times past tall buildings, always careful not to be intrusive and look in windows. Most often, I marveled at the city lights. When I stopped being afraid of being away from my body I was able to let go and have fun. My dream world was a launch pad for out-of-body experiences. Deep yet alert sleep was the catalyst to merge with nonphysical environments. In my teens I asked my mother if she had flying dreams. She replied, "I used to have them when I was young." Although my mother could not expand on the subject, I felt we had similar experiences.

Many people share similar views that there is more to reality than they can see or touch. Psychologists might suggest flying dreams are a phenomenon created by the human psyche, to rise above the unrest of life's turmoil and conflict. The weight of the world is lifted when we can fly high above and compartmentalize the complex facets of the subconscious terrain. There is certainly a link between dreams and the human will to overcome obstacles. But people have an essence with a higher self linked to an energetic system operating beyond the borders of the physical world. My dreams gave me insights into other worlds without being asleep.

At 23 years old, I lived in a bungalow in West Hollywood California with my Akita Shepherd mix, Bruno. Early one morning I left to attend a college class. I returned in the afternoon, feeling tired. Bruno was sleeping cozily on the bedroom floor, so I lied down on the bed. As I started to drift between wakefulness and sleep, I had the feeling I was detaching and rising up above my body.

Soon, I drifted away and found myself with Bruno on the sidewalk outside the bungalow. He was playfully running around me. I motioned for him to come to my side when he ran into the street. A car was coming at a high rate of speed. I ran to his side, grabbed his collar, and effortlessly lifted Bruno out of harm's way, as the car passed through me. Not realizing my strength I flung him into the air, spinning in a cartwheel above me. Suddenly I was awakened by Bruno excitedly pressing his nose against my face, panting like he had just run a long distance. He was a mellow dog, not prone to affection, and his behavior was very unusual. I felt we had met in a co-located environment between physical and nonphysical worlds.

In another out-of-body experience I flew above a large area with tall trees surrounding a lake. I began to descend toward a path winding through a grass field. Where I landed, couples and families with children strolled and played nearby. There were no concrete paths or modern buildings. Women were in long formal dresses, and men were wearing top hats with waistcoats and black jackets of the early 1800s. They carried themselves to the manner born. As I observed them pass by me, I felt invisible, as if no one was aware of my presence. I felt like I had stepped into a living museum, watching the unfolding scenes in another time and place.

In another transcendental event, I flew over a sun crested horizon with green rolling hillsides and arrived at a city. I landed in an old, narrow cobblestone street lined with Tudor-style buildings, its wood and stucco glowing in the dawn light. The street was empty except for a man standing nearby smoking a pipe. I turned to him and spoke with an English accent, "Excuse me, sir, do you know what year it is?" He looked at me puzzled, smiled, and replied, "But, of course, it's 1903."

In yet another event I walked along a huge ancient wall made of rocks and concrete and gazed across green rolling hillsides bordered by forests. Inside the building, my mother and father wore clothing reminiscent of the early medieval period. Tears streamed down their cheeks. I knew immediately they were full of torment for many losses in their lives, and I was one of them. War was a common theme in this world. I was overcome with emotion, a deep sadness I could not escape in that time and place. I burst into tears and returned to my physical life with profound sadness.

In another experience I stood in a field looking at billowing clouds above me with pockets of blue sky as far as I could see. Focusing on the sky, my feet lifted off the ground and I began flying toward the clouds, merging with the lower layers as I passed through them to the higher clouds of lesser density until I was above the clouds. Ahead, the blue sky looked windswept with ripples and whitecaps. I realized I was not flying into the sky but toward a vast ocean. Moving across the sea were three ships sailing in a formation—an aircraft carrier, a destroyer, and a frigate huddled together—churning water spilling off their bows, forming urgent wakes as they plowed at speed. An eerie feeling came over me. It was not hard to imagine what task they would undertake, to either threaten or destroy. I was overwhelmed with empathy for the souls aboard the ships as I felt their fear and anger for the terrible destruction they faced. Within a few minutes, I woke up, immediately struck by the profound feeling that I had been a witness to a long, dark history from my perch in the sky.

Transcendent dreams can represent immersion into the worlds we come from before life—where we leave our armor behind—the physical identity, the personality, and the ego are stripped away to experience the spiritual aspects of the self interfacing with multiple nonphysical environments. These realms reflect the array of unfolding synchronicities. We may explore a timeline to which we have access, or we may interact with changing environments shaped by thought energy. Becoming unified with the whole enables our navigation of the whole. There may be hints of our personality, ego, or emotions in dreams, but they are no longer the dominant features of self for they have no useful role in nonphysical realms where the energetics of our system takes over. People are uniquely suited to enable a seamless interplay with the nonphysical. Therein lies a clue that our dreams can take us into the nonphysical and put our essence in the driver's seat. We may not unhook during sleep and merge with nonphysical environments. Dreams can also unfold within our mental, psychological, and spiritual landscape influenced by unconscious memories, emotions, and desires, generating the vivid dream events we sometimes remember.

The sleep cycle is where our essence acquires adaptive resources to deal with the tensions and stresses of life—to experience our wholeness and return to our bodies renewed. In simple terms, sleep helps us clean the slate, heal the body, and restore the psyche—to recalibrate the physical, mental, psychological, and spiritual aspects of our being.

Whether dreams are good or nightmarish, they can offer messages and insights into our deepest desires or enlighten us with windows into our inner world conflicts. Dreams can reflect the wonders and joy of our existence or they can be marred by the uncertainty of struggle, pain, and isolation, mirroring our sadness, anger, and fears. Dreams can certainly evoke more questions than answers. Sometimes we dream and remember. Other times we dream and forget. But we can often feel a part of a larger adventure as we test the frontiers of our existence. Waking up with memories from other worlds can fill us with wonder and mystery. We might return from an amazing dream to find ourselves questioning its reality and, at the same time, hoping we'll find our way back.

THREE

Actors on the Creative Stage: Awakening Our Awareness of Who We Are

Our essence gives us the capacity for discernment well beyond our intellect and knowledge, offering insight and intuition into the stuff we're made of—energy beings operating in accord with the Larger Field and our nonphysical family. The most important aspect of our humanness is our essence, the sum of what and who we are, representing the vital link to our energetic counterparts. The result is greater fulfillment and happiness. To deny our essence is to lose sight of ourselves and become vulnerable to the lure of materialism. My biological father exemplified this. As high-school sweethearts and then as newlyweds, my mother worked long hours in secretarial pools to support him through medical school. They dreamed of a better life ahead of them. As he became a successful doctor, he detached from the family he was building. He was abusive, and they separated when the youngest of their four children was one year old. A string of girlfriends and four wives later, he remained emotionally isolated, never able to form a lasting bond with his wives or five children. My relationship with my father began and ended with conflict. At times we tried to resolve our differences but never achieved a lasting connection. In the randomness of my parents' union, I inherited our crippled relationship. Perhaps not random at all, but a synchronicity of what was meant to be. What I eventually realized was an inheritance of existing connections to people with whom I share a history beyond my present world. These thoughts arose from my understanding of the people who significantly influenced my attitudes and behaviors throughout my life. Many of them made beneficial contributions and others, like my biological father, had a negative impact on me that I eventually learned to see as contributing to understanding myself. The story of my father draws a clear parallel to my own story, except that I changed the course of my life where he did not. I became willing to let go of old obstacles and conflicts, leading me to create a fulfilling life. Once I made a decision to change, my higher self came forward to guild me.

My father's role as a medical doctor represented the positive features he saw in himself—a confident, likable, and charismatic person with power. While his career allowed him to develop the lighter, beneficial qualities of his being, he also disowned his dark characteristics. The more he denied that side of himself, the more the shadows dominated him, triggering conflicts in his personal life and leading him to isolation and loneliness. My father never learned how to access his essence to contribute to his relationships. Tenderness and closeness begins with the resolve to be present with our essence. It's up to us to make the connection.

For him, change was not of interest. He was very successful in his business life. As a doctor, he helped many people and was happy in that role. His doctor's life was full of purpose and meaning. But at the end of the day, he returned home and was unhappy.

When I was a child, he could become fiercely angry and throw tantrums that escalated into confrontations between him and my mother. It wasn't until I was 17 years old that the extent of his abuse became clear to me. In 1978, my girlfriend and I finished watching a movie and she left the room. I turned and stared into her dresser mirror, remembering what a friend had told me—that my eyes were like looking off the edge of a cliff. As I searched for the cliff in my eyes, a sudden memory rose from my unconscious and hit me like a wave. I saw myself as a crying baby when I was scooped up by large hands and I heard a voice yelling, "Shut up!" I was tossed into a crib and bounced off the mattress into the wooden lattice designed to keep a baby from climbing out. I experienced the feeling I would die. I drew a breath and let it out slowly, saying to myself in the mirror, "That happened." I felt no emotion as the flashback uncovered information previously unknown to me. The insights were oddly empowering and gave me a sense of purpose to look back at my early life. My biological father and I had unfinished business.

The flashbacks of our karmic history was a first step to resolving our conflicts. In my interpretation, karma is the unfolding of thoughts or actions creating positive or detrimental outcomes, linking the past, present and future. I also view karma as an unfolding synchronicity. Karma is especially evident when agreements align between two or more people—thus, karma can connect seemingly unlike energies on a parallel path for good or bad. Karma had brought my father and I together over the course of our lifetimes. We had been soldiers in wars that had significant consequences on our evolution. The thing about karma is staying power. Karma can remain a formidable force supplying the present with subconscious information and thus altering the course of personal evolution. Where my father was concerned, I viewed karma as a disconnection between the ego and the essence. As my father's ego ran his life, his essence was forgotten. Ensuing conflicts abounded. He never allowed his essence to retake its position so that his ego could balance its power between reason and purpose. He lost sight of himself and brought his suffering home to his family. His place in my history was becoming more apparent. But to explore his role fully, I needed to find understanding in our relationship. On some level, I knew he was tormented by his own traumas.

It takes trauma to inflict trauma on another human being. In the unfolding of our karma, pain is relative. I sensed he and I would have to reconcile. Even if that was impossible, I owed it to myself to balance the scales of my karma with or without my father.

I was fortunate my mother had the strength to kick him out of the house and move on with four young children. He was a womanizer and prioritized his homes, cars, and boat. After he retired, he spent most of his time with the expensive toys he acquired with his wealth. For the rest of his life, he continued to struggle with being close to his family.

When grandchildren entered the picture, he reached out to be in their lives. My siblings and I saw him attempt to connect with his grandchildren. He got down on their level and played with them on the floor—something he never did with his own children. But for all his attempts to be close, he could not reach the children's spirit with real tenderness and love because he lacked a connection to his essence. At the end of the day, he went home alone.

He was a man who denied the fundamental part of himself, his essence, his shadows, and the will to know both. While he yearned to be close to others, he had lost sight of the ability to create deeper fulfillment that comes with human connections. He may have been born with caring, empathy, and love originating from his energetic family, but in life these attributes can be forgotten.

Where his family was concerned, he rejected his role outright. His life was smaller than it could have been. I often felt his yearning to break the bonds of loneliness and isolation. His fleeting personal relationships revealed a disconnection from his essence that might have brought him greater fulfillment. When late in his life he became ill, he finally settled down and spent the rest of his days with one partner.

My biological father taught me a lot about how people are indeed actors playing a part on a vast creative stage. We are immensely imaginative cocreators, but many don't know it. As creators, we are responsible for every one of our creations. Responsibility begins with observing ourselves, our experiences, emotions, feelings, desires, and behaviors and reporting to ourselves for the record.

With a mental record, we can keep track of the events and behaviors that make us why we are the way we are. Losing track is analogous to forgetting ourselves and forgetting the clarity, unification, and wholeness offered by worlds beyond. With those connections we gain enormous value from the spiritual wealth we have access to. What feeds us is connection, and when our essence is denied, we can succumb to spiritual starvation.

At times in my evolution I lost sight of my essence and sought to counterbalance my hunger with anything other than my essence. The acquiring of money, sex, drugs, and material possessions preoccupied me. I experienced disconnection from my essence and diminished the beneficial connections to my higher self and energetic counterparts. I became distant from people around me—my parents, girlfriend, and family members—disconnecting from the loving relationships in my life. I was focused only on my physical life and neglected my inner life, denying myself deeper connections, and ultimately denying the expression of my essence. When my girlfriend saw me drifting away from our six-year relationship, she understood she could not change me. Nor could my family. If they attempted to tell me their concerns, I shrugged them off.

For many years I allowed myself to be swept away by the lures of the physical world. What's wrong with that? Physicality is an impressive creation. It can retain our fascination and curiosity for a lifetime. Yet it is only one part of a larger reality influencing who, what, and why we are—human beings with access to the boundlessness of our essence, which in turn has access to the Larger Field.

Like other people, I experience what life has to offer. I have agreed to live in my body. I treat it well. I enjoy it. But the body is only a temporary suit that gives me access to the physical environment. The essence transcends physical and other environments. For all the adventures I seek, there is an imperative I place above all others to encourage the awareness of my essence—being grounded. Discipline, focus, and intent. Being lost in materialism is only a distraction. To remember we are more than our body we may begin to acknowledge our essence as the connective tissue to our energetic core family.

But when the essence is forgotten, we can lose sight of our nonphysical counterparts and become vulnerable to the lures that take us away from ourselves. The ladybugs, butterflies, and other childhood and teenage experiences offered me an awareness of the larger reality beyond, which was always present somewhere in my memories.

These early life events seemed ordinary at the time I experienced them until I undertook an investigation in later years—the events revealed extraordinary details of interactions with other worlds. Transcendental is a word denoting a nonphysical reality. While the physical universe is widely known to contain planets and stars in the vastness of outer space, the worlds I refer to throughout this book are nonphysical environments, where the association of interrelated energies or multiple selves representing our fundamental wholeness exists. We split off from our nonphysical family with the agreement of our higher self to experience life, so it is accurate to say we are a part of them.

Paying attention is about getting back to basics and reestablishing the fundamentals of our connection to our energetic counterparts. The clarity can provide a fantastic sense of confidence that no matter what troubling events occur in physical reality, we may find ourselves at peace in the playfulness of the universe. Each of us can make wishes on the wings of ladybugs to manifest our dreams. We can be present today, deliberately and with intent, opening doors to experience reality as it is leading by way of essence.

To know ourselves is to discover the worlds we come from before life, for they reveal the extraordinary events that shape our lives. We begin with the desire to explore. We cross the bridge to the recognition as we are, partly physical and nonphysical beings yearning to experience all we are. I sometimes wonder if I discover worlds beyond, or do they discover me? Do I happen to the stories, or do they happen to me? They are the unfolding synchronicities set into motion by the mysteries of existence.

FOUR

The Island Party:
The Woman in the Antique Dress

During an evening in 1973, moored in a Catalina Island cove, I could hear the raucous laughter of people at play in the cabana on shore, their voices echoing off the rocky cliffs surrounding the cove where I stirred restlessly on my father's boat. I was 11 years old, sitting at the chart table, leaning against the starboard hull, watching *Lassie* on a shoebox-size black-and-white TV my father had set up for me. The boat was named *El Tigre*, which was fitting for my father. In his early 20s, he had been surrounded by gangbangers in downtown Los Angeles with his best friend. They had tried to walk away. When one of them was shoved, my father turned fierce—and as if possessed, he charged one of them, knocked him down, spun around, and jumped on another one. My father fought them off like an angry tiger until they ran away. My brother and I learned of this story decades later while dining in a local beachside restaurant. The restaurant owner and my dad had been high school friends when the incident happened. He recognized my brother and I and recounted the tale with great enthusiasm. We were surprised to hear the story but it resonated. *El Tigre* took on a whole new meaning.

That night I was alone on the boat as the party noise reached my ears. My father, his wife, a friend, and a couple of dozen members of the cove—all yachtsmen from the California mainland—gathered together on shore.

The empty boats moored nearby floated on the glassy stillness under a crescent moon. There was just enough light to see gentle ripples in the water as the hulls bobbed slightly in the wake of the ocean meeting the island. I would climb down the boat ladder and swipe my hand across the water, marveling at the bioluminescence of living organisms glittering like the Milky Way, but I had grown bored. The laughter kept rising and falling like a fast gust of wind unsettling my ears. I was expected to go to sleep. After a day of snorkeling, hiking, and diving for overboard lines and equipment, I should have been tired, but I wasn't, so I decided to row ashore to join the party and check out the bustling excitement.

I climbed aboard the dinghy, set the oars in the water, and headed to the island. I knew the water well and easily navigated the other boats and rocks along the cove entrance. I left the dinghy on the pebbled shoreline. I headed up the beach until I found the path toward the cabana lit by a firepit, lanterns, and grills. Cigarette embers rising to lips cast a reddish glow on the partygoers' faces making them look wild-eyed in the heat of the night. I was intrigued and excited to be part of the fun.

The sound of wooden mallets smacking abalone echoed as people joyfully prepared the crustacean delicacy. Fish caught hours earlier were being cleaned and grilled. The scene was a festive celebration. Every person had a drink in hand as they exchanged rowdy laughter. Shortly after arriving, I ran into my father. He wasn't expecting me, but he was elated to see me when he poured what looked like water from a bottle into a cup and handed it to me. He said, "Drink!" I felt the eyes of everyone in the cabana turn their attention to me. I lifted the cup to my lips, drinking the liquid in a single gulp. The cabana erupted in laughter as a volatile fluid hit me hard. The potency of the liquid made me struggle to keep my composure. I was instantly repulsed—the hard alcohol assaulted my senses. But I forced myself to remain stoic and conceal my distaste for the vulgar substance.

I had my first swig of vodka and I hated it—and hated more the deception in which it was delivered. My father had blindsided me and made me the brunt of a painful joke. I knew I was taking a risk by going to the party but never expected this. As the vodka burned inside me, the laughter carried on. In the back of my mind I heard the word, "Leave." I headed for the trail down to the cove, slid the dinghy into the water, and began rowing back to the boat.

I tried to leave my shame and anger on the shore with the drunks. It was my own fault, I told myself, my curiosity got the best of me, and I got burned. I paid the price and returned to the boat. Oddly I did not feel tipsy or high, as if my body rejected the effects of the spirits. But the night was young, and the alcohol was not finished with me.

Back on the boat, I made my bed on a cushion beside the port dining table. I liked to sleep close to the center of the boat where there was less rocking if swells came up at night. I laid my head on the pillow and soon fell asleep. A few hours later, I woke up. The ocean was calm beneath the boat, but my stomach felt nauseous.

The air was still. No voices, no laughter. It was late. I knew all the people had returned to their boats. My father and his wife were asleep in the forward cabin. I slipped from the blankets and went on deck where my father's friend was asleep in the cockpit next to the tiller. Careful not to disturb him, I leaned over the railing until I could see the water below and threw up over the side of the boat. Immediately I started feeling better. I looked around at the perfect silence of the cove for a minute, returned below deck, and climbed back into my bed.

Just as I pulled the blankets back over me, I heard the soft voice of a woman calling my name, the gentle manner of her tone capturing my attention. I didn't move until I heard the voice again. I lifted my head until I could see over the dining tabletop. That's when I saw a pretty woman with long brown hair in an antique red dress sitting across the table. She appeared to be in her 20s.

I pushed myself upright. She was gazing at me warmly as if she knew me. Looking into each other's eyes, I wondered if I should know her. But I couldn't place from where. After a few seconds, I replied, "Yes," responding to her calling my name. Our eyes beheld each other and she gradually disappeared in front of me. I wanted to say more to her, but the moment passed. I lied down, pulled the blankets over me, and fell asleep.

The next morning my father asked if I was feeling okay. His friend had seen me up late throwing up over the side of the boat. I told him about the woman I saw sitting across from me at the galley table and how she wore an old-fashioned dress. He laughed at me and joked the boat had a ghost. For years after that, I never spoke about the woman to anyone, but I never stopped thinking about our encounter. I felt as though I knew her.

I tried to find a logical explanation. I had been feeling alone on the trip but that was common with my father, his wife, and friends. They were friendly and polite, but they never engaged me in conversation. Perhaps the woman in the antique dress was a figment of my imagination, generated by an unconscious need for companionship—a psychological manifestation to cope with my loneliness that night. Maybe the event was induced by the alcohol having a hallucinatory effect on me.

Was she a dream, I wondered? But I was wide awake during the visit. I clearly recalled the ocean breeze on my skin and the moonlight reflecting on the water and boat. The event was so vivid. My instinct was telling me that she and I knew each other, although she remembered me much more than I remembered her.

I felt as if she appeared to check if I was okay, make her presence known when I needed support, and send me affirmation of existing links beyond my present world. She was signaling me to look beyond myself and gather perspective of the view ahead.

Years later, I looked at the event through the lens of nonphysical understanding. I recognized an emotional connection between us. She and I cared for each other. The circumstances that brought us together in another world would only allow us to briefly cross paths in the present. Two beings on a parallel path might share destinies that began long ago in a timeline juxtaposed by the interplay of many worlds, for the bonds we form along the journey are not broken and can unite us. The role of our essence and higher self is without limits or boundaries, enabling us to interface with the Larger Field.

The woman in the antique red dress was of another realm. Though she wore a dress, she was not of this world. Where she resided in nonphysical environments, there's no need for a body, or what I call a physical suit. The suit we wear uniquely equips us to live in the Earth life system. Our body enables us to be on the planet, yet its unrealized capabilities include our essence, offering us the potential to experience who we are by learning about ourselves beyond our intellect, ego, and emotions.

FIVE

The Doctor: The Intelligence Within

We place great value on eating well, exercising, and taking time to rest and nurture our spirit, giving us the energy to pursue our dreams. Yet life's demands constantly test the limits of our capacity to remain in the zone. None of us escape being carried away by circumstances beyond our control—our lives become subject to high tension and stress that can overwhelm us. Our energy becomes depleted, our spirit feels low, and we struggle to feel rested and vital. The way home is fraught with disruptions when the weight of the world hangs on our shoulders. How we cope with the external forces determines outcomes. To regain stability, we talk to friends, seek healthy routines, and work on achieving balance in our lives. We intuitively focus on what is most important.

However, we can often overlook a vital aspect of building the core strength needed to manage stress. I'm talking about a fundamental value as crucial to our welfare as the air we breathe. When tended to, it acts as a connective tissue to our energetic qualities, providing stability and harmony within the physical, mental, and psychological aspects of our being, enabling us to rise above the stresses and tensions we face. Awakening awareness of who and what we are can help us overcome life's challenges by supporting us when we feel lost or stranded without a clear path. Awareness of our energetic system does not remove the tensions and stresses from the equation of life, but it shows us that difficulties don't have to weaken our bodies or spirits. Indeed, the trials and challenges we face can make us stronger when we recognize ourselves as highly resourceful and innovative beings, able to gain the advantage of our wholeness.

My father loved the ocean's biology, saying it was a highly sophisticated ecosystem populated by an enormous variety of microorganisms able to absorb and cleanse itself of impurities. We often met at the water to sail and swim—perhaps to be imbued by its wonders—and help us heal ourselves. In my early 30s, we prepared the boat as we often did for weekend excursions. This time we loaded the boat with enough provisions for a month and sailed to Santa Cruz Island. We planned to be on the water for the lunar eclipse that year. During our first few days on the island, we wandered the shores and hiked the chaparral hillsides, discovering indigenous species of plants not found on the mainland 25 miles away. Lava rocks eroded by millions of years of ocean and weather formed sculptural shapes, giving us the feeling the island was of another time.

On the day before the eclipse, we pulled anchor and sailed to the island's northern shore where we anticipated a better view of the celestial spectacle. As we navigated around the island, the weather seemed to conspire against us. A moist layer of clouds shrouded the land and sea. We arrived at our destination just as a heavy fog swept around the boat. As the sky turned gray, we gave up on seeing the eclipse and planned for a quiet dinner with some music and reading. After we finished our meal, I collected our plates and stood in the galley, washing and drying dishes. I looked out the companionway to the sky above and to my amazement there was a clear and brilliant star-filled sky. The fog and clouds had shifted over 25 miles away, forming a wall along the coastal mainland to the east. The starlight and rising moon appeared amplified due to the shroud of fog over the mainland that blocked the sky-glow from the city lights. It was a beautiful setting. The stillness of the crystal-clear air created its own glowing effect. I yelled to my father, "The show is on!" We grabbed blankets and made ourselves comfortable on the deck, awaiting the arrival of the eclipse.

The next few hours of celestial gazing became my most meaningful interaction with my father that revealed a connection far beyond the challenges we faced during the early years of our lives together. My father was not easy to know, and I believe he shared the same sentiments about me. For the most part, our communication hinged on misinterpretation and misunderstanding. It was challenging for him to be emotionally close to me, and I craved a connection with him. The uncertainty created constant friction between us.

By the time I was in my teens, he had identified me as a young man he could teach to drive cars and sail. He could rely on me to dive for lost anchor lines and overboard winch handles for *El Tigre* and other boaters in the coves we frequented. One day after an exhaustive effort working underwater on the boat, I surfaced and heard him say, "You're working so hard. I love you." It was awkward, and I felt a bit uncomfortable. It was uncharacteristic of him to express emotion, and I was at a loss for words.

We found common ground on the ocean. As we worked together to restore the boat, we seemed to do the same for our relationship. But unlike the boat, our relationship needed more effort than we could give. Our inability to experience a deeper connection imposed an awkwardness that left me feeling he was incapable of seeing the person I was. His work as a doctor was a subject that gave us common ground. But to reach him or feel reached by him took extraordinary circumstances. The tone of our relationship was set many years earlier during my parents' separation. After he moved out, I often begged my mother to invite him to dinner.

When he would come to dinner, he'd sit at the end of the table and talk about his day or make jokes only he would laugh at. Sometimes he never gave us a chance to talk. Once, when I was about four years old, I went to his side, picked up a spoon, and hit it on the table to get his attention. He turned and slapped my face. I fell down, crying. My mother became enraged, and I could hear her screaming and throwing dishes and tableware at my father. In terror I detached, staring at a dusty paint chip curled up on the linoleum floor. Then I heard the front door slam. He was gone.

She kicked him out to protect my brother, sisters, and me. But I continued to beg her for dinners with him, which always ended in some type of drama or confrontation, though he never hit me again. At school I made a drawing of my family at the kitchen table with a big black face above us, representing the fears experienced when my father was home.

When I was in my teens and 20s, our sailing trips showed that we could sustain relative ease for days. Anytime I opened up to try to reach him, the flow between us was disrupted. He'd shut down and become reclusive, which was how he managed his emotions.

Then a change occurred when we worked together to perform some kind of task. The raising of sails. The cleaning of a deck. The sanding of teak. The way to bring out the best in my father was through the one ethic he identified with most: work. If an anchor line detached or a neighboring boat lost something overboard, I'd put on a wetsuit and dive in without an oxygen tank. I was a fish. At least once a trip I'd search the bottom of the cove and remain there after finding the lost objects, oftentimes holding my breath for an extraordinary amount of time to show him how hard I was working. That always made him happy.

One summer, miles at sea, we were sailing to the Channel Islands. My younger brother was playing around with the dinghy line, and it became loose and drifted away. We hesitated to tell our father at the helm of the boat because we knew his reaction would be harsh. Before he could notice and start shouting at my brother, I redirected his attention by diving in and swimming the distance to recover the dinghy. He got busy turning the boat around, and my brother was spared. By the time I was back on the boat, he calmly told my brother not to play around with the line. I like to think my actions helped my father be resourceful. Rather than falling into an angry fit, he took stock that my brother and I were doing our best to be with him, even though mistakes were made. I was learning that my father could behave badly because he was trying to be in control. When I took control of situations his power seemed to diminish. I started being proactive in finding solutions he could not challenge. I noticed he was more relaxed and often asked for my help.

My brother and I were fortunate to have a strong mother and stepfather who, through their guidance, gave us the foundation of confidence, which was reflected back to my father as a measure of strength he had to respect. Yet he could still lose his temper. My older sister became a psychologist, and after talking to her, we concluded that being close to our father meant conflict. She used to say he had a limited capacity. That made sense and helped me let go and accept our relationship the way it was. I learned to move on. With this perspective I could appreciate our relationship and discover his best qualities. His keen interest in biology and medicine and his ability to joke and laugh made having a relationship with him possible. I also admired his willingness to help people in need. On several boating trips he was whisked off to the other side of the island when someone got poisoned by the spines of a fish or injured in an accident. He always kept his doctor bag on the boat and had become a resident hero for jumping to action.

There were qualities in him that I could appreciate, but we were on different paths. We continued to meet for day sails or overnight trips to local islands. Then the trip to view the eclipse in Santa Cruz happened. The weeks together were a turning point. I recognized the potential of a deeper connection between us. The island gave us a new vision of the relationship we were capable of having by getting ourselves out of the way, moving past the unrest of the conflicts that influenced so much of our earlier life and becoming our truer selves in the stillness of the ocean and the island.

The tone of that trip started pretty much the day we set sail. The 11-hour journey across the bay took us to a cove on the island's south side. In the morning we took the skip ashore to explore the island. We started out walking side by side, meandering further apart until our individual curiosities pulled us in different directions and we lost track of each other. Time went by without awareness of its passing. I occasionally looked around for my father. I'd see him walking aimlessly across the beach stopping, bending down to pick up a rock or shell, and gazing into his hand as if opening a dialogue with nature itself.

The man who ran his life with calculated and meticulous order was nowhere to be found as he shuffled across silver sands quietly absorbing the natural world from the vantage of another world. He stepped outside himself to cognize an awareness far exceeding his ordinary modes and discover consciousness in the indiscriminate objects he encountered. In those moments, the rocks, shells, and crystal sands spoke to him, and he spoke back.

I watched my father in an intimate communication with worlds beyond, like a child discovering new wonders with a fantastically present state of mind. I had never seen my father behave this way, and I began to recognize the calm-natured person he was capable of being when the fierce struggle to control his world was out of the way. Yet he could dismiss the wonders and beauty of moments like this when the day-to-day stresses of life on the mainland came bearing down.

We had sailed to the island and put that world behind us, immediately falling into a zone, taking in the wonders and moving well beyond our usual selves—transcending the illusory materialism that guided so much of our relationship, replaced by the interplay of our larger selves unfolding on a unique stage of the natural world. In the days leading up to the eclipse, we found common ground.

When the sky opened up and the eclipse happened, we sat on the boat deck, pondering the Earth's location in the galaxy—the shifting patterns of the sky captured our imagination. An odd glow saturated the vast expanse of space. Our vision reached deeper into the galaxy, the Milky Way becoming amplified many times its usual brightness. As we gazed in awe, the living system spoke to us. We listened and spoke back. Time did not stand still—it ceased to exist in our reality. In this setting, our conversation began. I asked my father if he'd ever seen a miracle in the hospitals where he worked. He explained that he had seen patients who were not expected to survive, but they recovered.

He then told me one particular story. As an obstetrician-gynecologist, he was chief of obstetrics at USC Hospital and ran the woman's county hospital in downtown Los Angeles for most of his career. His practice also included seeing male patients who were housed on other floors.

One day an older man in a coma was transferred to his hospital from another L.A. hospital. According to the man's doctors, he was not expected to survive. But the man ended up in my father's care. My father focused on rehydration for five days and conducted daily evaluations. He made a diagnosis to surgically remove a blockage around the spleen. The operation went well, and days later the man awakened angry as hell. He told my father his children came to visit him when he was in the coma. They bickered and argued about how they wanted to save money by transferring him from an expensive private hospital to the downtown county hospital. They discussed how the remaining estate would be split among them. The man was comatose, yet he could hear the conversations around him as if he was fully conscious. When the man was well enough to leave the hospital, he climbed into a taxi and went straight to his attorney's office. My father said gleefully that the old guy still had a few good years left.

We had a big laugh. I asked my father how the man could hear his family's conversations while in a comatose state. He replied, "I don't know." In silence, we wondered how it could have happened, being that the man was so close to death. But my father had gotten used to such events. He learned to accept the mysteries he encountered during his career as extraordinary events that defied logic and reason. During his nearly 40 years of medical practice, he saw people survive when they should have died and die when they appeared to have years ahead of them.

My father was a man of science. His favorite instrument was a microscope, which he used to explore the biological world and life's building blocks. Yet he acknowledged that medical science, for all its advances, could not provide insight into the larger questions of life and death.

"We are under our own power," he said.

I responded, "Maybe it's our choice when we come to life and leave this world."

"Maybe. I don't know," he replied.

As a doctor, he took his patients to heart as he honed and perfected his craft with all the ingenuity he could manifest, including working with intuition as a diagnostic skill. He told me he reached a stage in his career where he could open the door to his waiting room, look into a patient's eyes, and have a good idea of the ailments afflicting them. His first impressions of a patient's health began with his intuitive diagnostic process, having gained the advantage of insight at a glance. Intuition gave my father a starting point to apply his doctor's knowledge and instrumentation technology to confirm or reject his suspicions. Most of the time, he explained, his first impressions were correct. It's no wonder his patients traveled from all over the world to see him at his private practice. He helped many people during his career.

I asked my father where his intuitive abilities came from. He shook his head and said, "I never thought about it." His reply always stuck with me as innocent. He spent his life studying medicine and perfecting his skills as a healer. But he was unaware he was accessing his energetic counterparts to help his patients. For all my father's intuition, he was first and foremost a man of science who believed strongly in validation and proof. Yet he was also well aware of the unseen phenomena in the human condition, which played a role in his patient interactions.

His experiences revealed windows into the mysterious worlds

he dealt with daily—the seemingly invisible connections to forces beyond his comprehension but not incomprehensible to the innate knowing of his essence. He could look into the eyes of a patient and gather critical information. Yet he was unable to explain the role of his energetic system in overseeing his interactions in the physical world. His patients benefited from his Earth-based knowledge as much as his otherworldly intuition. By placing one foot in the physical world and another foot in the nonphysical world he gained a broader understanding of the care his patients needed. Thus, he accessed his nonphysical system's organization and intelligence to perform his job. He achieved a high degree of intuition and insight through unification with his energetic family providing clarity.

The role of his energetic counterparts offered vast resources, supporting him through direct communication—a gut feeling or a voice in the back of the mind, guiding him through the blind spots in life, and helping him adapt to the ever-changing environment.

My father's remarkable abilities are not uncommon in people who spend their lives developing a skill set, becoming an authority in their respective fields, and displaying talents exceeding their education. They learn to function through the intelligence of their energetic system. These professionals become highly successful business leaders, sought-after experts, and teachers in their fields.

During the 1950s my father learned surgical methods at Chicago Medical School and moved to California to teach the latest techniques. As a teacher, he was by the book. As a doctor, no book could give him the edge he gave his patients by tuning in to his system. Occasionally I visited my father at the Los Angeles County Hospital. I watched him come out of surgery with blood on his smock and a smile on his face. The nurses and administrators couldn't wait to tell me what a great father I had. Loved by the staff, he was happiest at the hospital where he found his greatest sense of purpose and fulfillment. I rarely saw that side of him outside of work and never with his family. His role as a doctor brought out his best and happiest self.

Through interactions with my father, I discovered that people could transcend boundaries for intuition and insights from nonphysical environments and apply them in the physical world. The greater access an individual has to the clarity of worlds beyond, the greater they are perceived as creative, talented individuals. But intuition and insight are inherent features of human beings, regardless of their training. It certainly helps to have an education when pursuing a career. Desire and determination go a long way to discovering unification and wholeness that allows the flow of synchronicity to instill itself in the life process. For all of my father's talents that may have seemed random, he functioned with the role of his energetic counterparts, offering vast resources to provide the timing and execution of intelligent life-changing decisions.

As the evening proceeded that night on the island, I was getting to know my father in a new light. Soon the Earth came into perfect alignment, shielding sunlight from the moon's surface until it turned a cool orange-yellow hue as the total eclipse unfolded before our eyes. The background of stars and the Milky Way became amplified by what seemed 10 times their usual brightness. Our vision reached deep into the galaxy where an odd glow saturated the vast expanse. In those moments from our diminutive location in the physical universe, we were filled with a powerful wholeness, indivisibly unified with worlds beyond. Two of us as a single observer. There was nothing to do, nothing to change, nothing to become. There was only being.

For the rest of our lives, until my father passed away at 69, we could recount those hours and be carried to the furthest reaches of the multiple worlds and recognize we were a part of something much bigger than ourselves. We found our place in spiritual worlds. We would always have that clarity to remind us of our essences coming together with the understanding of why we are and who we are. However, after the trip, I continued to encounter our conflicts on the mainland, and I came to accept our relationship took many forms.

SIX

Tank Hill: The Perfect Order of Synchronicity

I began to understand synchronicity as a universal force at play. We might believe our lives are a series of unrelated coincidences. Yet events can remind us of the fantastic ways the world works. We may think of a friend we miss and suddenly they call us. We might seek a job that seems impossible to get. Suddenly, the door opens. I once needed to move from a home. I took a walk in the city to clear my head and passed by an apartment with a uniquely shaped window. I said to myself, that looks like a place I could live comfortably. A week later a rent sign appeared in the window. I moved in and spent four happy years there. That is the playfulness of synchronicity unfolding in our lives. Every tic of the clock, every interaction we make, every thought we create, every instance from birth to the perceptible now has brought us to this precise moment by way of synchronicity. Life is the embodiment of synchronicity, connecting the infinite interplay of our essence unfolding in worlds present and beyond.

So much is unknown in our world. Humanity sets sights on the exploration of space, the oceans, and the mysteries of the genetic and molecular worlds. The sciences lead the way to explore new horizons. But the physical world is only a fraction of the experience we are already having in the Larger Field.

What appears *solid as ice* can become *liquid as water* can further become *gaseous as vapor.* Apply that analogy to the apparent "solidity" of the physical world. Does that give you any insights into how molecules are not stagnate or isolated?

The year I received my driver's license I enjoyed the newfound freedom to discover adventures away from my family's home. One such adventure was on a local hilltop my friends and I called Tank Hill because of the old derelict water tank from the 1940s which had been recently removed. The narrow drive up the hill let out on a rounded hilltop the size of a small horse corral. At night I could stand there and look at the city lights spreading out for miles across the valley below.

The fantastic view stretched all the way to the surrounding mountains. My friends and I enjoyed exploring the area and considered the hill our private playground. One day we found some discarded 2x4 and 2x6 boards in various lengths. It sparked my imagination that something useful could be created. I returned the following weekend with my hammer and nail bag and started working, laying out boards like a puzzle until

I had designed a roughly 8x8-foot deck with one-inch spacing between each board. I braced the backside with a subfloor to stiffen the surface before dragging the finished deck to the edge of the hillside overlooking the valley. I used the claw of my hammer to dig holes and set smaller length boards as pillars in the ground for the deck to rest on at the edge of the hillside. I built the deck strong enough to carry the weight of as many people as could fit on its surface.

My friends and I made the trip up Tank Hill during the evenings to enjoy the views. On moonless nights the city lights gave us just enough ambient light to see each other's faces. The deck was a perfect place for stargazing, hanging out, and drinking beer. My friends and I talked about things high schoolers talk about and laughed into the evening. Suddenly, I was compelled to step to the edge of the deck—which I had positioned to be slightly raised off the sloping hillside—and this gave me the feeling of floating over the valley below. I stood there perfectly still, taking notice of the city lights twinkling in the distance. I recalled my astronomy teacher lecturing about the phenomena of twinkling lights, caused by molecules filling the air and falling in and out of alignment in fractions of a second between a viewer's eye and the light source. The twinkling captured my thoughts as I concentrated intensely on the distant lights.

The voices of my two friends in a conversation behind me faded into the background as if they were moving away from me. Something odd began to happen. I saw a distinct pattern of lines like a vast curtain rising from the horizon. The lines appeared to form mathematical squares of a grid pattern, stretching upward until blanketing the entire sky.

I was absolutely spellbound by the grid. I perceived it was growing larger, expanding and moving steadily closer to me. Or was I moving closer? Simultaneously I began hearing a high-pitched whirring noise, like thousands of cicada insects in increasingly thunderous harmony. My curiosity piqued as the grid merged and enveloped me. My sense of self and location was indistinguishable—the whirring increased a thousandfold as the remaining part of me mixed and unified with the field of energy. I felt a last sensation of density melt away as if gravity no longer existed. I went with it and allowed myself to be carried with the field I had encountered.

At some point I heard my friends yelling far off in the background. Their alarmed voices intensified as if we were moving toward each other. A second later, the whirring noise subsided and everything reverted back to normal. One of my friends appeared at my side looking shaken, stuttering, "Dude… we were looking through you." I looked at my other friend sitting behind us. He was also visibly shaken and mumbling indiscernibly. He avoided eye contact with me for the rest of the evening. Our minds were unable to grasp or articulate what had happened, and after that night we never spoke about the experience even though the three of us continued to hang out at Tank Hill.

Back then, it was difficult to describe what happened. I experienced an event beyond my teenage comprehension. Yet it changed me, confirming things were not as they appeared. It caused me to revise my perceptions and beliefs about the nature of reality. What is physicality, and what is energy? Are they the same mutable forces—creating, dismantling, and recalibrating structures in a field of ever-transforming consciousness? What is consciousness? I was learning that everything is consciousness, and nothing is indistinguishable except by the immutable boundaries of human perception. Perhaps on Tank Hill I was part of an extraordinary synchronicity, a cause and effect of improbability putting me into a precise alignment. Where on Tank Hill hill did I go? Scientists have confirmed particles can disappear and reappear, but where do they go? In the years ahead I came to understand the extraordinary event of that night. I had become unified with a field of energy, reduced to my essential state beyond the body. Pure energy. Essence.

Imagine if you placed a flower on your bedside table, cleared your mind, entered a meditative stance, and focused on entering the flower. At what point would you cross the boundary of solidity to transcend physical molecules and merge with the energetic field of the flower? The Tank Hill event was my first experience revealing that the physical environment appears solid only from a physical point of view.

Human beings have speculated for millennia about the

existence of nonphysical worlds. Validating nonphysical worlds begins with a willingness to explore who we are beyond our beliefs and sciences, and to be open-minded about the capability of human energetics. Humanity is on course to discover the true potential of human spirit through the experience of the Larger Field.

Many people I've met over the years report transcendental events they cannot place in the context of their lives. Their otherworld experiences fill their lives with the understanding they are not isolated and alone. They have gained the benefit of access to their essence and experienced a deep sense of fulfillment. My stories of the ladybugs, butterflies, and Tank Hill awakened a deep inner knowing, a recognition of worlds unfolding beyond me, inspiring my further exploration and discovery.

For the writing of this book, the physical and nonphysical aspects of a human being represent a whole entity. Wholeness means existing connections to energetic counterparts. Our essence is the point of entry, offering a continuous exchange of information between the physical and nonphysical worlds.

Being aware of our higher self and energetic system's roles can foster interaction with them, yet we are in constant interaction with other dimensions of reality, whether realized or not. Insight and intuition are examples of connecting beyond ourselves to gather information directly from the nonphysical. All people can attest to the experience of intuition, but we most often take for granted our intuitive abilities to interface with the nonphysical as a means to navigate our daily lives and, in certain circumstances, as a necessity for survival. As to the events of Tank Hill, I conclude the experience was full of insight into who I am and what I am capable of. The event revealed inherent resources in my ability to cross boundaries. To dematerialize and reconstitute in a visible form is a testament to the nature of the environment we live in. What appears solid as ice becomes liquid as water, further becomes gaseous as vapor.

I can only attempt to interpret with my limits of intellect what is effortless for my essence to show me, to literally encounter and experience the Larger Field from the density of my present location here in the Earth life system. This chapter illustrates the remarkable synchronicities throughout human reality. Each of us is inexorably linked to the Larger Field that enables us to experience far broader capabilities than we can imagine. That is our birthright.

SEVEN

The Man from Melbourne: The Adventure Within

Sometimes we become so overwhelmed by the stresses and tensions of life that we lose sight of ourselves, which is akin to losing touch with our essence. We may feel hopelessness and deem ourselves unworthy of our dreams. We must look inside ourselves for core strength from the part of ourselves that knows no boundaries, existing without struggle or conflict, able to steer us to greater clarity. Our essence offers us the capability to link with our higher self. Wholeness helps us overcome obstacles.

In the early 2000s, I met a man from Melbourne who returned from a two-year excursion in the Australian Outback. Before his adventure he told me he had never lived outside the city. I asked how he fared in the Outback, considering the many extreme dangers he faced. His first year was hard, he explained. Afraid and uncertain, he prepared himself to live in an environment where he was unsure how to survive, but he had committed himself to the extreme conditions. There was no turning back.

He was dealing with extremely challenging conditions before his trip to the Outback. He told me he was unhappy and unfulfilled without a purpose in his life. He had lost sight of his dreams and was no longer inspired by living. His failing self-esteem made him feel like giving up on life. His trip to the Outback was an attempt to break the negative pattern and find a path to recover his well-being.

During his first year in the Outback he faced daily life-threatening dangers. Waking up alive each day was an accomplishment that far outweighed the depressing insignificance of his past. In the gauntlet of the Outback, he had put himself far outside his comfort zone. To compensate he focused his attention inward in the pursuit of survival. As he faced his fears head-on, the waves of dismal thoughts subsided, eventually replaced by the challenge of discovering his strengths. He brought many prejudices into the Outback and found himself testing their usefulness as he was forced to examine the limits of his beliefs. During the day, he kept moving to hunt for food and stay aware of predators and the poisons he could encounter in the plant, reptile, and insect worlds. By his second year, he was connecting with something much bigger than himself—his essence. By tuning in, he was connecting beyond himself where he could have greater access to his higher self. He became acclimated to the environment and fine-tuned his skills at hunting wild animals, finding drinking water, and foraging for edible plants. If he could make it in the Outback, he could make it anywhere.

The dangers of the Outback no longer haunted him, nor did his past. He was discovering previously unknown senses, enabling a heightened awareness by unifying his once disconnected and fragmented self with his essence. He'd walk on a trail when a sudden tingling sensation entered his body, warning him of a dangerous obstacle ahead. Slowly he'd pull back a low-lying tree or push aside a bush to find a venomous snake or spider. He started to rely on feelings and sensations in his body to manage the onslaught of threats. He described his transition to a broader awareness as a shift from seeing himself as separate from the living wilderness to merging with it, opening a dialogue, and bonding with the world he explored.

To sustain that kind of focus day and night, he cultivated a state of mindful clarity, enabling him to access nonphysical resources. The most important aspect of his adaptation came from being grounded in direct contact with transcendent sources outside of sensory, intellectual, mental, and technological processes. His interactions with the nonphysical were the acquired skill he unconsciously sought. In this stance, he learned to detect subtle changes in the environment, the traces of footsteps or slither marks, and the odors of creatures.

He also learned to dissolve his long-conditioned attachments to fear by focusing only on the feelings, intuition, and senses he needed to function in the present. As he got himself out of the way, he freed himself to experience greater awareness. In this stance, his immersion filled him with a lightness of being. Living in the Outback became his second nature, and he began to feel joy, something he hadn't known in a very long time.

His wilderness experience was a meditation in every step he took. He put aside the old self, enabling a seamless union with inner resources, thereby allowing him to turn and pivot with flexibility from moment to moment, giving him the advantage to see ahead of the curve and anticipate what was needed to remain safe.

The man from Melbourne had learned the skills endowed by natural abilities to link with his system. And yet he likely had no conscious knowledge he was communicating with other realms. He started with a singular objective—to find purpose in his life. Inadvertently, he acquired the organization and intelligence from his nonphysical counterparts. Insights, intuition, and all-encompassing awareness gave him a clear advantage. The two predominant aspects of his identity—his physical and nonphysical self—merged to become a unified whole. Thus, he learned to operate beyond himself, beyond all the self-doubts and uncertainties that once plagued him. He had opened doors to the vast resources available in the nonphysical. He attained clarity in the undivided wholeness of himself.

His encounters with the local Aboriginal tribespeople gave him a model to emulate. The Aboriginals were already in touch with their energetic counterparts, which enabled them to thrive and adapt to the harsh conditions of the Outback. He witnessed the Aboriginals in a conscious dialogue with nonphysical environments as they fostered interconnected relationships with the physical world. Through them, he discovered living things share the same nonphysical origin. Like many tribal communities around the globe, the Aboriginals understood the interwoven nature of spiritual and human worlds, unifying their wholeness as a universal feature of their humanity.

When he first entered the Outback, his goal was to survive the many dangers he faced. He exceeded his goal by learning to thrive. By the time he left the Outback, he had conquered his fears. Acting from his wholeness and a learned belief in himself gave him a balanced perspective to meet the challenges for the best possible outcome. By integrating physical and nonphysical worlds, he functioned with greater agility to execute his goals. Like an actor, he poured himself into his role and, in the process, fostered existing connections to his counterparts.

I asked if he knew the origin of his intuition and the warnings he felt in his body when in danger. He shook his head and replied, "Can't say." The man from Melbourne entered the Outback with only a rudimentary plan to hunt and camp. Out of necessity, he got in touch with the unifying characteristics of his being and the remarkable synchronicity of his adaptation unfolded.

He went into the wilderness to find himself. Ultimately the wilderness was never his destination but merely a place to test his resolve and discover what he needed to become fulfilled and happy. His story sheds light on how we can interact with worlds beyond us without intellectual knowledge. For the man from Melbourne, achieving wholeness was a triumph. In a purely physical context, he became an authority on how to survive in the Outback. In a nonphysical context, he gained understanding through direct, personal association with the Larger Field.

The story intrigued me about the countless ways people walk the path and how our transcendental nature is an innate facet of the life experience—even if unaware of the nonphysical, we can operate on both sides of the bridge between the physical and nonphysical as a common feature of our human energetic characteristic.

It's fascinating to think the nonphysical is on hand to engage our resources with or without our conscious recognition, and we benefit just the same. The man from Melbourne spoke with a keen sense of worlds beyond. He learned to listen to his inner voice guiding his every thought and movement, enabling him to move with ease through the thick and thin by the fortitude and strength of his being. Many people have made the journey inward by stepping outside their comfort zone and engaging in situations seemingly out of their depth, where they've learned to thrive in the face of extreme adversity. Taking the journey inward doesn't necessarily require entering extreme environments like the Outback. Inner discovery can occur anywhere—in nature or in cities. In the greatest sense, the wilderness is all around us at every moment of our lives. Every day people take the journey without leaving their familiar surroundings. Whether people enter the forest or remain in the comforts of their home, they have the opportunity for self-exploration and discovery. The man from Melbourne teaches us that the journey to wholeness is available to anyone willing to put their essence in the driver's seat.

EIGHT

Bob: Discovering the Light Within

The power to make unwavering decisions from which we change the course of our lives begins by accepting who we will become when the old obstacles are no longer present. A resolute commitment means learning why we are the way we are. Along the journey, our essence gives us the clarity to discover where we come from to help us see where we are going. Knowing sets the stage for greater purpose and happiness in the present and the future.

My father certainly accumulated some negative karma resulting from his abusive behaviors toward me. I am also responsible for its creation. In our past lives, my father and I shared links to dark history from other times and places from which we brought conflicts into the present. We both had negative karma and in the laws of attraction, fear attracts fear, anger attracts anger, and pain attracts pain, like magnets of opposing fields. We were two beings playing out our karma on the stage of life. How I behaved as a result of my father's abuse became my karma. And how I eventually changed myself became my karma. In the Larger Field there are no limits to the karma we create.

But karma can remain hidden until circumstances thrust it to the surface. Karma has staying power, remaining a formidable force like an echo from the past, supplying the present with information. As a teenager I lived an extremely destructive lifestyle. I used drugs. Stayed out all night. I took my friendships for granted. I manipulated my closest relationships to ensure their trust in me. In my teens, when I saw the vision of my father's abuse, I focused on him intensely and unconsciously sent a thought signal into the Larger Field. The echo of my thoughts reached my father's psyche. He had been struggling with guilt for years, as would any human capable of sorrow and regret. Within days he called and asked me to lunch. He looked uncomfortable and preoccupied when we met. That wasn't unusual for him, but this was different. He was stumbling for words when he finally said out of context, "It was a difficult time for me. I wasn't getting along with your mother." After a moment I realized he was talking about events that took place during my early childhood.

He tried to say he was sorry for his behavior toward my siblings and me. He tried to explain how difficult things were back then. I felt he was making an excuse and not holding himself accountable. I had never been thought of as an angry young man by other people, likely because I had become good at controlling my feelings and keeping them locked within me in a balance between repression and acts of destructiveness, such as running from police. Anger rose up inside me as I watched my father battle his demons to overcome them with the truth. I was not ready to hear it, nor was I ready for resolution. I shut down and became reclusive just like he was known to do. Both of us were still too detached from our essence to be effective at uniting.

My life during those years was anything but honest. I had picked up a marijuana habit and found the lure of the high to be just the thing to avoid dealing with the pain of trauma. My interest in finding a tranquil alternative to pain led me to discover other drugs to avoid dealing with my shadows within. Karma, it seems, was playing its hand in who I was becoming as a person, and I was mostly detached from my essence making me vulnerable to the lures of physical life.

At age 18, I was out driving one night in a little Alfa sports car when I ran a stop sign. The police pulled behind me with lights flashing. I knew I had a warrant for a moving citation that year, and I didn't want to deal with it. I made a snap decision and drove away, and a chase ensued. I drove hard and fast before entering a neighborhood and headed to a dead end. I spun my car around when the police caught up. Our cars collided. I was in serious trouble. I was put in a jail cell for three days without human contact. My parents hesitated to bail me out because I had been in trouble repeatedly and they were unsure what to do. When they finally picked me up, we started working on a plan to prevent me from going to jail. Suddenly I was in survival mode. The three days I spent in confinement were eye-opening. I never wanted to spend another day in jail, and I desperately needed to change my life. I wrote a letter to the judge overseeing my case, saying I was responsible for the events that night and was doing everything I could to turn my life around, including entering a rehab program. In the following days I found myself in a spiral of fear and distress over the situation I created. A forbidding and relentless anguish afflicted me every day. I felt I would carry the pain for the rest of my life. The events had brought me to an impasse, shattering the facade of self-deceit and exposing shadows from the dark corners of my being. I was sure I was dying. Then I had a dream one night. I was aware of being away from my body when I opened my eyes in a beautiful room with pillars and a bright light which seemed to come from everywhere. I found myself in a courtroom facing a judge. He wore a white robe and had long white hair and a beard. I felt a wonderful presence as if the environment was filled with caring and love that settled and relaxed me. The judge firmly spoke, "You can only judge yourself." I had the distinct feeling I was being watched. I turned around and saw an orb of white light suspended near the ceiling. I felt a strong connection to the light, as if we were linked to each other. This was a direct encounter with my higher self. Within a moment I woke up feeling a wonderful, comforting warmth and ease all around me. The terrible feelings of dread and fear were gone. I experienced a powerful sense of calm and a major shift in perspective. I knew everything would be okay, even if I had to go to jail. Later in my life, I understood the environment I entered was a stage created precisely for what I was ready to see and needed to hear at that time. That is one way the nonphysical works. The experience had life-changing implications.

The encounter with my higher self was a turning point. I had given myself permission to begin rectifying the karmic disorder that got me into trouble. I had become willing to connect with my essence to take me from where I was to where I wanted to be—resolved and free, thus helping me form a bridge to my system in nonphysical environments. I was learning to come to terms with the karma I had created as a result of inflictions suffered by karma, and was transforming negative karma into positive karma. I was starting to remember what had been forgotten. I was learning who I was, where I came from, and most importantly at that time in my life, why I was the way I was.

The rehab program revolved around structured days, including a support group and a schedule of classes in various subjects to build a healthy routine. The director of the program was a dignified man in his 40s named Bob. He wore neatly pressed button-down shirts and slacks. Bob always carried a clipboard and took notes during his busy day. He seemed to be everywhere in the building at all times. A man of few words who led by example, his presence earned the respect of his coworkers and the patients. He was a strong-looking guy who walked tall. Everyone liked his passionate caring energy.

One day I discovered something about Bob that surprised me. His shirtsleeves were rolled up, exposing violent-looking spider web tattoos in murky ink covering his elbows. I looked at him differently, as if his tattoos symbolized a dark and brutal past. I learned from another counselor that Bob had been a member of the Hell's Angels. He was in and out of prison and killed a man while in confinement. By all accounts, Bob's karmic debt was likely to ensure a life in prison. His future prospects were grim. While behind bars, Bob had reached an impasse. His fate was hanging in the balance when he made a decision to face his shadows and uncover his essence to change himself. Maybe the hard reality of life in prison set him straight. He had enough of living in darkness. To make a transformation, he would have to assume responsibility for his criminal past by looking inside himself and accounting for his self-created conflicts to learn why he was the way he was. He would have to manifest an unwavering determination to sever ties with the violent lifestyle of his old self as a member of a biker gang.

Bob's conscious decision enabled him to let go of his past and focus on a purposeful life. By becoming aware of his essence, he acquired greater access to his higher self and the vast inner resources of his system to stay the course. During his court appearances, the judge in his murder case had determined sentencing guidelines based on Bob's criminal past. Bob had other plans in mind when he spoke to the judge about his vision for the future. The judge believed him and took a chance.

After Bob's release from prison, he and the judge met once a year for lunch. I'm sure the judge was proud of the way Bob had rehabilitated himself and was leading a life of purpose helping others turn their lives around. Bob was a model human who taught the value of inner clarity and the benefits of a fulfilling life. He had made a decision at the core of his being to accept with resolute determination who he would become when the old dark ways were no longer present. Unwavering and steadfast, he closed the chapter and never looked back. By becoming a better person, he contributed to the betterment of humankind. For Bob, unification equaled a series of synchronicities that changed his life. This is the ultimate recalibration of karma. Bob's spider web tattoos were reminders of the instability and violence from whence he came and a springboard to where he was going, like indelible marks telling the story of his rise from darkness.

Bob had a quiet manner and the light in his eyes revealed the strength of his spirit. He changed his life with a decision and transformed himself with powerful resolve, and thus opened a treasure trove of opportunities to reestablish links to the beneficial resources from his system's immense organization and intelligence. He inspired me to reach beyond myself for existing connections and become a better person.

NINE

Fear on the Mountain: Regaining Access

As human beings, we are capable of experiencing fear, but our essence knows no fear. Fear can only be experienced in the physical world. Fear begins in the mental and physiological landscape and we can feel it in the body. When overwhelmed by circumstances beyond our control we learn to face our fears, which can offer the benefit of removing distraction and allowing for wholeness to come into play. Wholeness is the connection to our energy system, providing the foundation to work in synchronicity with the playfulness of life and overcome obstacles. That is our birthright.

I saved the life of a friend during my middle school camping trip to Dark Canyon in the Sierras in the summer of 1974. On the second day of the trip, I was hiking with two friends, Matt and Danny, along a river flowing through the canyon from the hills above. I was the more confident hiker, having lived for years in the hills where I grew up, so I took the lead as we stepped over boulders and rocky outcrops until we were a couple of miles from the campground.

On the way back to camp the three of us forged a path along a hillside above the river. After a few hundred yards we were walking on a steep hillside that merged with a cliff. We were careful to keep our distance from the cliff's edge as the difficult ground pushed us into a narrow passage.

The terrain was slippery and unstable, and our adrenaline spiked as we navigated a steep rocky incline. Soon we began to feel fatigued with the sun's heat. Feeling a grave sense of responsibility for our safety, I became determined to center myself on the goal of getting us back to camp, focusing inward to become totally present in the moment.

Ahead of us, a fallen tree blocked our path with its trunk resting over the cliff. We had no way around except to climb over. As I approached the tree, I tracked the steep terrain with firm careful steps as my friends followed close behind. As I reached the tree, a sudden feeling made me turn around just in time to see Matt walk into a blanket of leaves piled high on the ground. He began to slide toward the cliff's edge. Our eyes met. The panic on his face turned to terror. I reached for a branch on the fallen tree with one hand and reached out to Matt with my other hand. We grasped onto each other as I pulled Matt to safety. The moment happened simultaneously in slow motion and in the blink of an eye.

Years later I reflected on my luck of seeing Matt step on the leaves and begin to slide toward the cliff. Had there been any delay in my actions Matt's fate would have changed. Possibly Danny's and my fate, as well. Had Danny reached for Matt he could have been pulled over the cliff with Matt. Turning around and reaching for his hand was the synchronicity of intuition, an impulse entering my thoughts from beyond my physical location. As I tuned in, my instincts became sharper, increasing my awareness due to the exchange of information from the nonphysical. Tuning into our essence means tuning into the vast resources of our energetic system in nonphysical environments.

In later years I realized how synchronicity was created by other worlds behind the scenes influencing every step we took. I saved the life of another human being that day on the cliff by linking with my nonphysical counterparts, and thus a synchronistic event occurred. At the time we were just three buddies sharing an adventure. The close call was just a part of the day's experiences. After a short moment to catch our breaths the three of us continued our journey, grateful to be alive and looking forward to catching up with the rest of the group at the campsite.

About 20 years later I found myself in another perilous hiking situation. It was on the same trip to Santa Cruz Island with my father to view the eclipse. While anchored on the island's north shore, I put food and a camera into my day pack.

I planned to hike to the highest hilltop at the center of the island, which was only about a mile and a half away in a straight line from the cove. My father and I rowed the dinghy ashore and hiked into a narrow arroyo to follow the creek through the surrounding cliffs. We soon parted ways. He headed back to the boat and I hiked on.

The arroyo darkened in the shadows where sunlight did not reach. I stepped over boulders, gradually ascending into an increasing thicket of chaparral. It soon became apparent the terrain ahead was impassable. This low-lying area in the nook of the canyon was damp and overgrown. Water filtering down from high above soaked the landscape, accelerating the growth of vegetation. There was no way forward without a machete to hack my way through.

To my left side, about 10 feet away I observed an extraordinary formation. A smooth, dark igneous rock from an ancient lava flow had laid a smooth pavement. From ground level it looked like a path reaching the upper hillsides. I could not see where the flowing rock curved out of sight, perhaps 50 meters above. It was steep yet looked passable.

I was a confident hiker with a good sense of direction, so I started climbing the route out of the arroyo. As I climbed higher up the lava flow, patches of sunlight dotted the canyon above. I was about 100 feet high and climbing fast. Soon the walls steepened, and my pace slowed to a full stop as I could no longer find foot and hand holds to climb.

There was no way out. The wall was too steep to climb down. My confidence waned, and I felt fear overcome me. I had reached a tiny ledge, leaning into the rock, and contemplated my next move. My fear increased along with my pulse. I froze with uncertainty. The instincts I brought with me were diminishing by the fear consuming my thoughts. I had to make a decision quickly. If I stayed put it would be hours before my father realized I was not returning. A rescue would have required a helicopter from the mainland. The sun would set in five hours, and I could grow exhausted and slip off the rock.

I took some long deep breaths and made a core decision to put the fear aside. I had to clear my head and find a way off the rock. At that moment I felt a wave of calm come over me and a voice in the back of my mind saying, "Forward."

I scanned the rocky surface above me and spotted a small cave about 30 feet away. If I could get to the cave, I would be safe. I studied the details of the slab I was leaning into and reached for a small edge barely within arm's reach to get a handhold for leverage. I slowly pulled myself to a position where I found another handhold just within arm's reach. I continued to scale the rock with deliberate movements aimed at inching my body upward. When I reached the cave, I knew I would be okay. I had risen above the fear and transcended the obstacles on that mountain. My confidence had waned for a moment, but my intuition kicked in and led me to safety. Becoming consumed by the fear meant risking it all. Instead, I focused on accepting the circumstances I put myself in and drove myself to overcome them. Climbing the rock was possible. But the risk I was willing to take meant I would need to access the full accord of inner intuition, my instincts, and even the best of these might not be enough to get past unforeseen dangers. A slip off the rock wall would likely have ended my life. My intense focus put me into a stance that awakened my intuition and sharpened my instincts to overcome the obstacles, enabling the full capability of my nonphysical resources. The nonphysical is always there. On that day it offered me the clarity to find a way out.

I emerged from the steep rock with the certainty I had overcome a close call. I moved to the cave to look inside. There was a sandy floor just big enough for me to rest on, but I was too pumped with adrenaline and still had more hiking to reach the highest peak at the center of the island. Ahead of me, I saw pathways through the thicket of chaparral, thanks to the island's many deer and wild pigs making the terrain passable. As I moved off the ancient lava flow, the hillsides came into view, the sunlight now shining on my face. Within two hours I was standing between the north and south sides of the island gazing at ocean whitecaps as far as my eyes could see. I felt a great sense of accomplishment knowing I had been given another chance to experience the beauty of life.

During the winter of 1991, I experienced another feat of survival. I rented a place in an area known as Conundrum outside a small town in the Rocky Mountains. I would put my cross-country skis on and enter the forest, sometimes in heavy snow. Spring was the best time for backcountry skiing, after the avalanche chutes had cleared off the mountains above. I woke up one morning to a sunny day, gathered my skis, and headed toward a large meadow surrounded by steep 1,500-foot-high mountains. Before entering the meadow, I scanned the chutes for remaining snow and ice that could cause avalanches.

The risk of entering the meadow with chutes full of snow and ice is extreme. My intuition was telling me there was danger ahead. But the chutes looked clear, indicating they had already released their winter buildup. I observed a thick blanket of snow, maybe 20 or 30 feet deep, covering the meadow and the river that ran through it. Before I entered the meadow, I scanned the mountains one more time to make sure the chutes were positively clear since the last storm a couple of weeks earlier. The spring snowmelt was underway. The avalanche zone was clear. I saw no apparent danger. I moved forward cautiously, each step sliding a couple of feet on my skis across the snow-packed meadow. Skiing in the backcountry had its risks, but the adrenaline producing rewards were worth the risk and I picked up my pace.

For the next hour I enjoyed great skiing, the day seemed perfect. Suddenly that changed when I felt my legs spreading apart involuntarily. Directly beneath me a crack formed a few inches wide that opened into a crevice between my skis. I could see the river far below and hear the trickle of water in the spring thaw. I froze in place and my life flashed before my eyes. I knew the crevice could grow wider and swallow me if I continued forward. Adrenaline filled my body as I focused intensely on my next movements by slowly and very carefully side-stepping away from the crevice until the snowpack gradually felt firmer. I slid my legs forward inches at a time, aiming my skis for the edge of the meadow.

When I reached the safety of the tree line, I kicked the ground and screamed to purge myself of the remaining adrenaline in my body. Once I settled down, I started making a mental record of how it all went wrong. What might have happened if fear had taken control of my mind when I was standing over the crevice? What if I panicked and rushed to the safety of the tree line? That could have proven fatal. No one knew I was skiing that day. I imagined a hiker finding me after the spring thaw a month later. To what degree intuition played a role in leading me to safety off the field was clear. But listening to my intuition that morning could have prevented the incident altogether. Yet I overlooked it and entered a known danger zone. It was not a well calculated move, but I willingly took the chance. By ignoring my intuition, I was effectively ignoring the messages from my higher self and the protection I could have gained from paying attention.

I was determined to experience an adventure that day. My excitement thrust me out the door. It was a decision weighed against the risk I was willing to take. Everyday, we make choices about the risks we take. On a subconscious level, our intuition lets us know the risk of traveling in a storm or driving when we are tired. Life is full of calculated risks. Should I, or shouldn't I? We accept responsibility with every decision. Sometimes we play it safe. Other times, we push the limits. On the day I skied into the backcountry I put my intuition aside and played my hand. That time I survived, but I could have lost my life. By the time I was standing over the crevice, the message returned loudly. If I had experienced an extreme fear reaction, there could have been a breakdown of connection to nonphysical resources. But I acted to promote intuition, sharpen my instincts, and direct my actions to resolve the conflict. In this case, I got myself back in line with my energetic resources after I was in serious trouble.

The three stories in this chapter illustrate how fear can obstruct the connection to our essence and energetic counterparts. The decisions we make every day put us into a world of probabilities. We know intuitively that discernment can keep us safe. In every step is risk weighed against the odds. Knowing our limits is analogous to listening to our gut, allowing synchronicities to unfold. We all have voices guiding us—our energetic counterparts attempt to keep us safe throughout our lives. When we tune in, we can overcome the paralyzing effects of fear and create new pathways to wholeness.

TEN

Samantha and Fifty:
Communicating with Animals

All living things possess their essence as a vital link to others. We may make judgments about the limits of another being. Our essence makes no such discrepancies, as it speaks well beyond the intellect and ego. It functions without our conscious awareness and acts to unite us freely, without reluctance. The relationship between our essence and our nonphysical family reveals extraordinary connections to the worlds of the living and beyond. But fear can only have a role among the living, and its power over us can diminish our connections to each other and become a handicap to what should be a seamless accord of communications between the worlds we operate in.

Growing up with horses, dogs, and cats taught me some hard-earned lessons about building a foundation of trust leading to intuitive communication between people and animals. Some of the best teachers in my life have been the animals I've grown up with. They've shown me how to get myself out of the way to become present in an interspecies exchange. Being in their lives means I become present in my own life.

Animals are far more tuned into nonphysical environments than we can imagine. I have three dogs who make me slow down a little bit every day to enter the worlds they occupy, showing their effortless connection to worlds beyond.

My family always had pets. I grew up with a Boxer named Mitsey and a Great Dane, Samantha. At six years old, I gripped a leash with all my strength on my first dog walks with Samantha. Occasionally she took off running. I'd find myself sliding down the sidewalk at the end of her leash until the weight of my little body was just enough resistance to bring her to a stop. I earned her respect by never letting go. She'd wait for me to get back on my feet and allow me to walk her home.

A few years later, I roughhoused Samantha, pulling her front leg in an attempt to take her off balance. She understood I was teasing her. I wouldn't let up. I grabbed her ear with one hand and yanked her leg with the other as I pushed and pulled her. I was testing her to see how far the game could go. I was just playing, but in hindsight it was very unkind of me. After a moment passed, Samantha snapped at me, sinking her upper canine into my lower lip just enough to draw a little blood. I was stunned. She was telling me to stop teasing her.

I knew about being disciplined by my parents. They had a

knack for delivering a clear message when needed. Samantha's message was decisive—she spoke to me in no uncertain terms. After the bite there was a moment of silence. She just stood there. I felt her saying, "I'm sorry, I had to do it." I had confused her, made her feel helpless and she responded. I felt guilty and deserving of her lesson. Embarrassed by my actions, I kept our exchange a secret. When my parents saw the injury on my lip, I told them I bumped it. Samantha had taught me a lesson. I never teased or hurt her again.

She forced me to look beyond myself to understand her communication. I heard her on a fundamentally deeper level, essence to essence. As a result, we formed a stronger bond. We may have spoken different languages in the physical world. In the nonphysical, we spoke the same language. We met each other in a new light and formed an understanding beyond our present world. Samantha was already operating with clear links to the nonphysical. Her actions helped me explore my own nonphysical connections, adding immeasurable meaning to my life. We found our common ground, unifying us with the clarity of brighter realms. Having animals in my life is a constant reminder of the playfulness of the universe.

Growing up, my favorite horse was a colt with an old soul. He was a handsome Appaloosa named Fifty-Fifty for his contrasting white and dark spots front and rear. Fifty lived with our pony, Benji, and quarter horse, Penny, in the barn across the street from my family home. Fifty was fun to ride because he was responsive, energetic, and sensitive. I'd bridle him in the corral. To mount him I positioned myself close to his flank, placed my hands on his back, and pushed off the ground, throwing my leg up and over him until seated in a position close to his mane. I rarely used a saddle and almost always rode bareback. I thought saddles were unnecessary and limited the connection between horse and human.

The saddle made sense for long rides by making the journey less tiring on my back. Bareback just put us into the zone—lighter, freer, and in touch with each other. I'd guide him with the reins or use a soft leg in his side and we'd head into the tall grass and rolling hillsides dotted with old oak trees as far as I could see. Spotting deer in the distance was one of my favorite pastimes. We walked right up to them, far closer than they would have allowed if I was alone. On Fifty's back I could disappear in the union between horse and human, blending into the landscape.

I'd signal Fifty to catch up to the deer and we easily merged at their side, the sound of swift hooves clapping the Earth, the rapid breathing of animals flat out across the landscape. Our intense movements were tempered by an odd stillness enveloping me as if I had entered the world of the deer and horse.

Riding during the full moon was a great treat. We'd follow the moonlight on a familiar trail along a row of houses at the edge of the community before turning up a steep hill and heading into open space. During late springtime the trails were like corridors surrounded by six-foot-tall grass I could see over from my perch on Fifty. One night we passed the neon blue light of a bug zapper dangling from an overhang of a house. As we turned and headed up the steep trail, I leaned close to Fifty's neck to balance myself and make my weight easier to carry. Nearly cresting the top of the hill, I heard the sound of the bug zapper echoing off the hillside.

Fifty lowered his head as if searching for something on the ground and simultaneously exploded into a trembling mass of terror so intense my legs lost their grip, and I nearly slid off his back. I tightened my legs and gave a tug on the reins. But his fear reaction was just beginning, and within an instant he was reduced to a mass of wild energy. He spun around on the trail and ran straight down the hillside at a terrifying speed. For all my will and riding ability I could not restrain him. His fear was total, the connection between us was lost. One thousand pounds of out-of-control beast running, tripping, barely keeping his body on his legs as he carried me, terrified, atop his back. At any second he might fall and roll over, crushing me. It felt like the wild ride went on for an eternity, his inertia increasing down the steep descent until we leveled off at the bottom before I could regain control and calm him down.

I had seen Fifty lose control before, but nothing compared to this. One time I had him at a full run on a trail that let out into the street near my home. I leaned back and gave a gentle pull on his mouth to make him slow down, but he kept on running and my attempts to reach him made no difference. As he ran into the street, I could feel his legs slipping on the pavement. Finally, using all of my ability, I was able to stop him. Sustaining the link can become challenging or impossible when anxiety or fear interferes with the connection beyond us. It's not uncommon for horses to walk up on rattlesnakes and become disoriented by fear, especially if they've been bitten before.

Fearing for my life that night with Fifty, I too was caught in a rush of terror and struggled to save myself. But I never broke the connection to my system—to the contrary, I reinforced it by maintaining my focus with all my will and eventually reestablished the connection with Fifty. I was able to get Fifty's attention by reinforcing the link to my nonphysical counterparts and reestablishing an intuitive connection with him. He was nervous and twitchy for the rest of the ride home as he let me guide him back to the corral.

We consciously or unconsciously use inherent abilities to interface with nonphysical worlds where vital communication creates interconnected relationships in the physical world and fosters synchronicity. This is our essence at work, crossing the bridge in a continuous exchange between worlds and helping us connect with people and animals. The intuitive exchange is always available to us thanks to the connections we share in the nonphysical.

ELEVEN

Good and Bad Friends: The Proverbial Gut Feeling

Our essence is the ultimate instrument for taking measure of the happenings in our lives, offering the foundation for our instincts to flourish and our gut feelings to tell us the truth. In all situations we learn to rely on our intuition to make discernments about the situations we find ourselves in. While our essence may be present within us, we may not be present with our essence. The benefits of being tuned in with ourselves far outweigh the miscalculations and blunders of losing sight.

How often do you meet a new person and immediately feel comfortable in their presence? Likewise, you can meet people and experience an uncomfortable feeling. The proverbial gut feeling draws us in or repels us as a fundamental intuition, an innate knowing guided by our essence. Our links to other realms mean clarity.

Listening to our gut feelings can tell us a lot about the situations we find ourselves in. Not listening can evoke regret for making mistakes that could have been avoided. We motivate ourselves to make better judgments the next time our gut speaks. But gut feelings can be especially tricky to discern during periods of emotional stress. At times, we can be overly preoccupied with life and don't pay attention to ourselves. Making sound judgments is about getting ourselves out of the way—our worries, frustrations, and fears—to enable greater clarity and tune into the messages our intuition is communicating. Learning to listen gives us the advantage of being present with our essence where intuition flows.

When we are young and inexperienced, we may become easily distracted and not savvy about listening to our intuitive feelings. Maturity gives us the opportunity to make better judgments by learning to fine-tune our instrument, which is the way we sharpen instincts.

In my early 30s I met an individual and immediately felt he had my best interests in mind. To this day, we continue to be great friends. There are unique connections I've made with family members and friends who have taught me about the power of making commitments with people who pose no limits to the expression of friendship—that is, giving and receiving with the core values of empathy and caring.

How did I know these people had my best interests in mind when I met them? It's accurate to say I was fundamentally tuned in, able to read the signs, and know good fortune when it crossed my path. They opened their hearts and showed me love. There's another component involved in bringing me together with special people. Curiously, when I introduce new people to those already in my life, they are well received by each other because connections are transferable between energies guided by similar values from their nonphysical counterparts. It wasn't always this way in my life.

When I was a teenager, my mother met a friend of mine and told me he did not have my best interests in mind. I eventually learned her instincts were right. Intuition gave her a view into the dynamics of his character that I could not see at the time. In another incident during my youth, my stepfather tried to warn me about a friend I met during a family vacation. My stepfather had only met the person for a matter of seconds but that was all the time he needed. Later, I discovered the person was not trustworthy.

Years later as an adult, I found myself aligned with a business partner whom I believed to be honest. We started a company in the automobile business, buying four-wheel drive Chevy Blazers from Arizona and Utah and transporting them to Los Angeles. After a few months I began to feel something wasn't right. We were generating profits and buying and selling more cars. The accounting ledgers looked fine, but something still didn't seem right. I couldn't put my finger on it. I heard a voice in the back of my mind saying, "Get out!" Within a few months I discovered he had lied to me and was using proceeds to pay off restitution on a fraud conviction case.

I worked for an herbal company in the 1990s. They were looking for opportunities and aligned themselves with a marketing company to sell herbal products to a well-established client base. I met with the owner of the new marketing company and immediately had a feeling he wasn't honorable. The feeling entered my body with a clear warning not to proceed. But as a junior level employee I didn't have the sway to warn my boss. He took the founder of the marketing company overseas and showed them how the business operated, from locating materials to production and transportation.

A year passed and things were going fine. The herbal company delivered a range of products each month, and sales were growing. Suddenly, disaster struck. A shipment of energy drinks was delivered a few days late to the marketing company. It was a one-time event and was no fault of the herbal company. Rather than make an exception or ask for a discount on the drinks, the marketing company used a clause in the fine print to dissolve the contract. The financial repercussions were a hard hit on the herbal company as it had to destroy over $150,000 of product. After that, I learned the marketing company used trade secrets to build its own overseas herbal company.

The ability to "just know" is seeing beyond ourselves with stunning prophetic effect. How often do we reflect on intuitive exchanges with people in our lives and say, "I was right," or "They were right"? Most people operate with the benefit of intuition at the forefront of every step they take. Intuition is innate knowing rather than absorbing information through interpretation or analysis. Intuition can be viewed as a thought in the back of the mind or an impulse so subtle we don't notice it pointing us in a specific direction. Intuition can also provide visual snapshots in the mind's eye, appearing like pictures or moving imagery as a visual flow of instantaneous data with real-time information to assist us.

Every act of intuition links us to the nonphysical by way of our essence, where the origin of gut feelings and insights guides our decisions and actions—offering us the advantage of connection. Our direct links to nonphysical counterparts are our birthright. It's when we're distracted by the circumstances of life and pulled by the sway of dominating emotions that we can become bogged down with the weight of the world, forget ourselves, and temporarily lose sight of our connections to worlds beyond us.

Reacquiring the links means determining to center ourselves with an unwavering stance to put aside distractions and make sound judgments even during times of stress or emotional preoccupation. Acting with information acquired from sources beyond ourselves is our energetic legacy and is as natural as seeing the physical world with our eyes or feeling warm or cold temperatures on our skin.

Crossing the path to interface with brighter realms can take place anywhere or anytime where we may access the resources of our energetic system. In my years of inner exploration, I have come to understand that my nonphysical counterparts are always there, always able to link up. Even when focused elsewhere, my interface remains fluid. While intuition and insight have huge implications for human interaction, they represent a common theme of human participation in the nonphysical. Intuition is other realms interacting through human thought, manifesting the clarity to see beyond the physical self where we acquire a broader view of reality to meet the challenges of physical life. Intuition can set the stage for synchronicity to unfold.

How do we foster intuition? We give ourselves a gentle reminder to look past the intellect and ego to see past our reflection in a mirror and remember the fundamental nature of being is the essence we are from a nonphysical origin. The simple task of awareness gives us the advantage of looking beyond ourselves where we may engage our energetic family. From that vantage, we can begin to lay the tracks for clear and concise feedback from our system. However, awareness isn't necessarily conscious. Many of us engage unconsciously without ever paying attention to our essence—we are already aligned with our higher self. Desire, determination, and intention to link up with our higher self is a starting point to greater self-awareness. But we must be willing to put aside distractions to get ourselves out of the way, including our old limiting paradigms, beliefs, fears, and anger, and make room for our higher self to play a role in our lives.

TWELVE

The Stolen Artwork: Investigation with Nonphysical Resources

The most present aspect of our being is too often overlooked during challenging periods. Finding strength within can help us resolve the forces outside us. Life will never fail to test us. It's our responsibility to discover our true potential by recognizing we are a part of a much larger self that can join us side by side on the journey to brighter realms. Our essence is the key to helping us manage the resourcefulness of insights and intuition from our system. Synchronicity is always present in the playfulness of the universe.

Eight valuable oil paintings were laid over each other on the artist's studio floor, rolled up like a carpet, and fitted into a five-foot-tall tube to keep the artwork safe for traveling. The well-known painter entrusted me with his livelihood, so I kept the tube beside me like an appendage, gripping it tightly as I began my journey from the small Rocky Mountain town where I had lived for the last year. I was taking the art to galleries and dealers in Los Angeles.

I had represented artists for years. The artist was well known in the art world and I was proud to have the assignment. The week of visiting galleries and talking with dealers was hard work. I was on my way back home to the Rockies to return the paintings and start my next assignment. At the airport I collected the tube at baggage claim along with my suitcase. I loaded the airport cart and wheeled the artwork out feeling good about returning to town safely with the paintings. I hailed a taxi at the curb.

After a 10-minute drive, I arrived at the apartment where I would be staying with my parents who were on vacation with their two friends, a couple I had known since childhood. As the driver opened his trunk to unload my baggage, I began heading into the building, a few paces ahead of the driver as I was excited to meet up with the group. The driver and I exited the elevator and continued down the hallway to my parents' unit. I knocked on the door and was greeted by my stepfather. We embraced and there was a great deal of hugs and kisses with the group as the driver placed my items near the dining area and left.

After a minute I noticed the corner of my suitcase against the wall. It was blocked by the dining table. I moved a few steps around the table to look for the tube. It wasn't there. I walked around the table. Nothing. I opened the apartment door and entered the hallway. Empty. I asked my stepfather if he had seen the five-foot-tall tube. He explained he only saw the driver leave the suitcase.

I took off running to catch the driver before he drove away. I caught up to him as he reached his car. He opened his trunk for me. Empty. He explained he had only picked up the suitcase and saw nothing else at the curb. I asked myself how in the world this could be possible. I ran back to the apartment, rushing to make a phone call to the airport lost and found. My parents and their friends were very concerned for me. The party suddenly came to a halt. We were all looking forward to relaxing and hanging out. Then disaster struck as I realized the tube was gone. I immediately excused myself to begin retracing my steps.

I returned to the airport to check the lost and found. Nothing. I headed to the taxi pickup spot where I took the tube off the luggage cart and placed it upright next to my suitcase. It was nowhere to be found. As I scanned the area, the trail went dry, but I knew whatever happened to the tube took place at the curb. The distress was consuming me. I focused on trying to solve the artwork's disappearance. I said to myself, "What is lost can be found," which calmed my nerves. As I studied the scene, I tried to recount my every move at the taxi stand where I last saw the tube of art.

I was tired after the long trip back from Los Angeles and

absorbed with seeing my parents and friends. My guard was down because I had arrived home and felt safe. I recalled turning my back on the tube to greet the taxi driver. The driver had stepped behind me to get my luggage and I assumed he had picked up the tube. I got into the car and heard the trunk close, thinking the tube was in the trunk. I made a mistake by not visually inspecting the handling of my items from the curb to the car.

Then, my intuition spoke to me. Maybe someone standing nearby saw an opportunity. The moment I turned my back, the tube went missing. I had let my attention drop for a few seconds and it was gone. I felt in my gut it was stolen. At that moment I took a very different stance. I began to pursue the artwork like a detective in a criminal investigation. I wanted to give the benefit of the doubt that someone, perhaps another cab driver, may have mistakenly loaded the tube into their taxi. I contacted the cab company and they assured me they would let me know if the tube was located or if relevant information was received.

I figured if another driver accidentally picked up the tube, they would return it. By the end of the day the cab company had no further information. Now I had to come up with more clues to prove my hunch. I didn't want to waste a minute. The day was getting late and I needed some rest. I returned to the apartment and told my parents and friends I thought the tube was likely in the hands of a criminal.

I felt the paintings were out there somewhere. To retain my composure would be necessary to pursue them. I committed every ounce of my energy to my goal. My thoughts had no other purpose but to work through the puzzle. When my parents and their friends suggested I file a police report, I said no—if word got out that the police were looking for the artwork, it might disappear forever. I wanted to conduct a quiet investigation on my own. Later, maybe I would involve the police. My parents and their friends did not understand my thinking, yet they respected my determination. They told me to be prepared for the worst—the paintings might never be seen again. They did their best to support me with ideas and suggestions, but I was determined to stay the course on my path.

I wholeheartedly believed there were steps I could take to recover the artwork. Beyond my beliefs was a certain knowing in my gut that I would get the paintings back. I believed at least there was a chance. I might prevail by immersing myself in a single-minded focus. To begin, I needed to discover how the crime took place. Only then could I begin to solve it. I looked forward to getting some rest and formulating a plan to find the thief. I needed to feel each moment and get in touch with a deeper part of myself to help me define a role I was not familiar with. I needed to become an investigator.

That night I couldn't sleep—my thoughts were preoccupied with the events of the day and the challenge ahead of me. I began a deep meditative relaxation exercise that slowed my heartbeat and enabled my mind to slip away and come back. I was interfacing with other worlds, acquiring intuition and insight directly from sources that represent my energetic core family in the nonphysical.

I thought about the taxi stand that day. I saw a long line of cab drivers waiting for travelers to arrive. A vision entered my mind of a cab driver getting out of his taxi and picking up the tube of artwork from the curb and placing it into his trunk. I saw this image like a film rolling in my mind's eye. The thief was a taxi driver. My hunch was becoming clearer. I considered this my first lead based on intuitive insight alone, without hard evidence. I felt a taxi driver had taken the artwork. I knew my plan must include all the taxi drivers who travel between town and the airport. My job was to get the word out to every driver in town.

The plan began to take form and it was simple. I would return to the taxi stand the next day and greet each driver and tell my story. As I lay in bed, I composed a pitch for the drivers. It went like this: "Hi, my name is Stephen. I lost a tube of paintings at the airport. It may have been accidentally picked up by one of the drivers. The paintings are not valuable except to me. If you hear of anything, please let me know." I would give them a number and tell them to have a good day. I felt a deep sense of relief. I had a plan I could implement first thing in the morning. With my mind relaxed, I fell asleep.

The next morning, I drove to the cab company to meet the

owner. I explained what happened and told him I suspected a cab driver may have driven off with my tube. He was a straightforward guy who told me he hired people from many walks of life. It wasn't out of the question that one of his drivers might have taken the artwork. There were drivers in his company who had criminal backgrounds. I told him I was reluctant to involve the police because I felt once they made inquiries, any guilty parties would keep the secret and I stood to lose the artwork forever. I asked if any drivers were no-shows the day after the artwork went missing. He checked his roster and commented that one driver missed work. He gave me the driver's name and explained he had no phone number or address. That wasn't unusual in his business, he said. He thought the driver lived down the valley in a small town. I thanked him for the lead and told him my plan to talk to his drivers at the airport. He said that was a good idea.

I left his office and headed back to the airport where I stood near the spot of the tube's disappearance. With a cool and casual demeanor, I started talking to each of the cab drivers. I gave my pitch and paid attention to the inflections of their voices and their eye movements as they looked on with varying degrees of interest. Some expressed concern. Most were receptive and polite. I'd smile with a nod and thank them for their time. I quickly realized my exercise was about building trust with the community of cabbies. I intended to make myself known to the entire town of drivers.

Over the next several hours I tirelessly devoted myself to the task. When I began to see the same drivers return to the line, I'd smile and nod and move on to those whom I had yet to meet. I wanted to be sure every cabby who made the airport run saw me multiple times to make a strong impression of the importance of finding the artwork. By the afternoon I had met many drivers. My next step was to speak to the driver who was a no-show at work that day. Maybe he knew something. I arrived in the town and found a pub. I met with a bartender and casually asked if he knew any drivers who worked in the upper valley. He pointed with his arm and said, "Yeah, first floor." Moments later I found the apartment and knocked on the door. No answer. I had the feeling I was at a dead-end and there wouldn't be any answers here. It was late in the afternoon and the sun would be setting soon. I headed back to the apartment for dinner with my parents and friends.

They noticed I was far away from my usual self. Thinking I was withdrawn or preoccupied by stress, they tried to be uplifting. But I was nowhere to be found. I had immersed myself in unceasing meditation, internally focused, taking the steps to visualize my goal and yet remain detached, consciously letting go of the artwork and creating space to keep myself balanced. By remaining flexible I could use the tension to foster ongoing communication with my system. At this time in my life, in my early 30s, I had not yet given a name to my energetic system. I had put myself in touch with nonphysical realms, able to acquire intuition to keep me on track as I aimed at my objective. In my stance I was working full-time, 24 hours a day. To my parents and their friends, I may have looked far away. Yet I was the most present person in the room, methodically tuned in to every thought, planning my next interface with the community of taxi drivers and living the role of a relentless detective focused on recovering the artwork.

That evening I walked around town, watching cabby after cabby drive by, looking at their faces for clues. I got two clear insights from this process. The person I was looking for was a male, and he was close by. On the third day I returned to the taxi stand at the airport and saw new and familiar faces. I met a cabby I had spoken to the day before. He asked if I had any luck. I told him I was still meeting drivers and getting the word out. He smiled and said he hoped I would find my artwork. I felt like I was making progress. I had made myself known to most of the cab drivers in town and I felt their empathy and support. I knew these people had a network with a reach beyond their roles as cab drivers. I hoped the story of the guy who stood at the airport taxi stand was spreading around town. I wanted everyone to know about the missing tube of artwork and my determination to get it back.

Another couple of hours passed as I continued to meet new drivers. A driver pulled forward with a face I had not yet seen. I gave him my pitch and caught an unusual gaze that made me feel like he knew something valuable to solving my problem. I engaged him longer than the other cabbies, telling him in detail about the lost artwork and why I needed it back so desperately. I thanked him for his time and we parted ways with warm smiles.

As he picked up a ride and left the airport, I felt I had made a connection. I also felt the stolen artwork was close. By that afternoon I was sure I had met all the drivers in town, and quite possibly I had met the one driver who had the answer. I had no other evidence than my intuition telling me I was close. It was time to return to the apartment and settle in for the evening.

By this time, my parents and their friends had watched me come and go for days. They'd smile and say, "Wow, you're working hard. We're sorry you can't enjoy your time off." Weirdly, I was enjoying myself. I felt like I was operating with resources I had never experienced, making connections within myself and the world around me. I was putting myself out there, being productive, and doing something different than my usual routine, giving me a profound sense of purpose. The personal benefits were flooding in. My work felt complete. It was at this point I decided to let go. The rest would be up to the universe.

At 7:30 the next morning my mother woke me up to tell me there was someone on the phone for me. I climbed out of bed, went to a barstool in the kitchen area, and put the phone to my ear. It was the owner of the cab company on the phone. He told me he had arrived at work minutes earlier, and as he pulled into the parking lot, he noticed a cylindrical object leaning against the outside of the building. He said it could possibly be the tube I was looking for. He took the tube inside but didn't open it. He asked if I wanted to come and inspect it.

I quickly dressed and headed out the door. It was a cold morning, a few degrees above zero, and I thought if the artwork was in the tube, it might be damaged due to the extremely cold weather. I arrived at the taxi company and met with the owner. He pointed to the tube in his office. I recognized it instantly.

I opened the top and looked inside, seeing the canvases just as I had packed them. They seemed untouched, and I thanked the cab company owner gratefully. I returned to the apartment with the artwork and received a standing ovation from my parents and their friends. They were amazed I got the artwork back. I admitted to them I had my doubts about recovering the artwork, but I never doubted my ability to do what needed to be done.

Later that morning, my first call was to the artist. I could hear his elation. When the artwork went missing, I sensed his doubts about whether it would be recovered. We met at his studio. He removed the lid and assessed the state of the artwork. We both agreed it would be better to wait half a day to let the paintings warm to room temperature since they had been in freezing temperatures and removing and unrolling them could cause the paint to crack and flake. As he placed the tube in his studio, he jokingly said he wouldn't have hit me too hard with the bill for the art. We had a good laugh as we shook hands and said our goodbyes. The timing was perfect—it was the last day of my vacation.

I spoke with the artist later that afternoon. He had removed and examined the paintings. They were in perfect condition and I was relieved. Three days earlier I had made a wish to find the artwork. I had devised a role for myself to become an investigator to get into the minds of the people who could help me solve my case—the taxi drivers, the owner of the cab company, and even the bartender. They all played a part—even my parents and their friends—in the recovery of the artwork. In the process, I discovered nonphysical worlds communicating to me with intuitive insight to help me reach my goal.

I also formed agreements with the people who participated in the recovery effort. While our agreements were not established by spoken mutual consent, they nonetheless represented tangible links from a nonphysical perspective. In this context agreements were formed between people through their transcendental connections to each other. Agreement was also formed with my higher self and energetic counterparts. The nonphysical plays a significant role in forming agreements between human parties, as they are created without the limits of physicality. Nonphysical agreements are the basis of frequently exchanged consensual or nonconsensual agreements.

The agreements we form may be nonconsensual, yet they can still hold us to the consequences of not paying attention to the intent behind them. When I inadvertently turned my back on the canvases at the airport, I created an opportunity for a thief to steal them. The intent of the thief formed an agreement that had both physical and nonphysical implications. Although I did not consent to the theft, I became vulnerable to a nonconsensual agreement.

I was not a victim, but I was vulnerable. I let my guard down, enabling my nonconsensual agreement to manifest and link me to the theft. In my pursuit to recover the artwork, I formed other consensual and nonconsensual agreements with the people who helped me recover the artwork: the owner of the cab company, the cabbies, and, crucially, the driver whose eyes I looked into and experienced a flash of intuition. I recognized he had knowledge and agreement regarding the artwork. I was able to engage this person and modify the agreement to include the return of the artwork. But all the players whose roles contributed to the return of the artwork also made varying degrees of agreements having nonphysical implications to help me reach my goal. The consensual and nonconsensual agreements I illustrate here can be applied to every interaction between all living things in nonphysical and physical environments in every plausible and seeming unplausible circumstance. But all interactions take place with the agreement of the higher self which acts as the seen or unseen gatekeeper and guardrail allowing or denying any adventures the human essence experiences.

Most people might call it pure coincidence. I call it an alignment of synchronicities set into motion by agreement. During my three-day investigation to recover the artwork, I was able to successfully get people aboard my train of thought to create an alignment with my agenda resulting in a confluence of cause and effect to move the needle and connect the dots on the physical stage.

As a result of the process, I achieved a state of wholeness. The nonphysical is always there, ready to link up and provide support. Days earlier, I started with a wish to recover the artwork. Wishes are the first rehearsal for our dreams. Dreams may not come true, but their vision inspires our highest enthusiasm, offering access to the available resources at our disposal. This is a story of fostering synchronicity by being present and enabling the vast organization and intelligence of our counterparts to guide the process.

THIRTEEN

House of Screens: Know Thyself

I often repeat that awakening awareness of our essence gives us the advantage of insight into where we have come from and where we are going. Our physical self may have limited knowledge of the questions to which we seek answers, yet our essence retains the intelligence of our energetic system, making it possible to explore what has been long forgotten.

Memories carry positive and negative emotions influencing why we are the way we are. When I was about five years old, I began experiencing a recurring dream. I walked on a forest path, turning and twisting past rocky outcrops and hillsides, before entering a meadow and stepping over a little bridge to cross a stream. I arrived at a small house made of screens. I removed my sandals and placed them neatly on a wooden platform and stepped up to a sliding door on my left. My dream stops there and I do not enter the house. Eventually, I became aware the dream included two other people who lived in the house, a woman and a young girl.

I would wake up in the morning with the memory of the forest path, walking over the bridge, and arriving at the small house. The memory was like an ordinary recollection, a fragment of a familiar remembrance as typical as other memories except for a few distinguishing details—namely that the dream repeated itself often for several years during my early childhood.

I could have accepted the dream as a fleeting glimpse in the landscape of my imagination—like so many mysteries of the dream world, to be disregarded by life's relentless push onward. I may have tucked the dreams away in the archives of memory. But the dream had struck a chord in my life and held greater meaning for me. The events on the path were so vivid, so real. With a thought, I was back in the forest, entering the fringes of that other world, curious about what I might discover. I was inspired to reminisce about the fantastic realms I'm a part of and ponder visions of a continuing existence beyond my present world.

I told a few friends about the dream during my teen years. In later years I told the story to significant people in my life. My descriptions were still limited to the walk on the path up to the house, but not the world inside the house. The sliding door was the barrier I could not see past. In my early 30s, deeper implications of the story began to enter my awareness. They included a general feeling of discontent, anger, and profound sadness.

The dream of walking on the path had been my first clue to guide me through the perilous challenges in the world where the story occurred. But stepping across the threshold meant that I entered a world fragmented by long-forgotten anguish more distant than the memory itself. It's said that time heals all wounds. Time does not heal wounds. Time merely places wounds outside of awareness, fooling us into forgetting our sorrow and pain. By discovering unfinished business, we can make reconciliation by severing the old dark links from the past. Only then can wounds be healed.

Soon after my realization, the door inexplicably opened. There it was, wide open and offering me a choice to enter or walk away. I chose to enter the threshold and immediately recognized the woman and young girl from my dream. They were my wife and child. Becoming reacquainted with their memory revealed trauma from that time and place. There were no cathartic emotions. What took place in the house began to filter in slowly—at first in glimpses. Gradually the stage became more apparent. Eventually, many new memories rose to the surface, and I learned of my conflicts in that lifetime. I had discovered extreme trauma there, but it did not originate from the people I lived with. The trauma belonged to me.

I discovered my wife and child from my past life were trapped by my conflicts, and were the recipients of my pain. Our life was consumed by the fracturing effects of struggle and discord. As a husband and father, I was unable to show care and love. I was temperamental and angry toward my family. I raised my voice. I subjugated them and made them feel subservient to me. The culture we lived in promoted a man's role to dominate his family. I was living according to the values of society, and I was raised by a father in that lifetime who acted to subjugate his family. My job in that time and place was terrifying. I worked in a military capacity and assisted in the political aspirations of leadership. I would spend long periods away from home conducting military campaigns. When I returned, I brought with me the traumas of war and inflicted my wife and child with my pain. The advent of conflict and unrest made our lives very hard. I made decisions that put me in a very difficult position in a divided political realm, and I carried out my agenda with little regard for the suffering I caused people.

My wife and child desperately tried to keep themselves from drowning in the discord and disunity. Seeing my role in that world was a tipping point that helped me understand how I hurt the people I should have cared for. My agreements in physical and nonphysical environments created a detrimental effect on my being.

Throughout my life, I had experienced conflicts from the unconscious circumstances around the woman and child. I was seeing the darkness in my past and beginning to understand the circumstances I created that enabled conflicts to return in my present life. I was learning how pain can remain dormant inside the mental and psychological landscape. It can be hidden from view—but not from the psyche. To deny the pain might help me compartmentalize and separate its effects to keep it out of sight of daily life, hidden in the deep storage of my inner world landscape. There it could remain outside my awareness. But I could not escape the unrequited emotions echoing a parallel theme between my past and present. It's easy to forget the past when focusing on the present.

In many ways, suppressing inner-world pain is necessary for survival, yet its very existence casts a pall on the journey ahead. A friend once said, "The love we withhold is the pain we carry." I was lost in pain. I began to recognize that the conflicts of anger and sadness were not the real me. Once embedded in my inner world, they took on a life of their own, acting on emotions and influencing the behavior, perceptions, and outcomes of my life.

Today, I view my dream on the path through the forest as one of many stories relating to other lifetimes that impacted my present life. This is not the first time I carried baggage across eons in the physical timeline. From the energetic perspective, the distance is a day's ride across the prairie of one world to the next, separated only by the perception of time and space when reality is one continuum of existence. An interesting thing occurred when I began to pay attention to my larger evolution. I began to observe myself as the creator of my destiny. In this context, I created everything about me, including, anger, sadness, fear, and the derivatives of emotional pain. Becoming aware of the obstacles meant becoming responsible for them.

This did not mean I could easily remove the obstacles. To do that I had to make decisions to sever the bonds and ties that linked me to the past. The responsibility was mine alone to clean the slate.

By recognizing myself in the dream and exploring its implications, I found awareness. With the knowledge came understanding, truth, and freedom. Nothing more was needed. In letting go, I closed a chapter and opened a new chapter in brighter realms. The person I am today is certainly due to the circumstances I created. Sometimes the question of who and why we are is revealed in mysterious ways through dreams. The answers are always inside us.

FOURTEEN

The Healer: Past Life Trauma Awakens

As an extension of our higher self, we humans have the capacity to heal old wounds and begin anew. The long-forgotten secrets of our being are certainly well known to our essence and our energetic counterparts—but to learn about ourselves, to truly grasp the understanding of where we've been and how our paths have changed us, means we are becoming aware. In the greatest sense, we share the same origin with our system, and therefore no one knows us better—as one cohesive whole—than they do. Sometimes we may experience snapshots of memories like a flash from the past. But memories are like dust in the wind. They can be lost in time and inexplicably become reconstituted in a visible form. We may choose to explore them further. It's up to us. When we decide to look closer, our system can watch over us every step of the way.

During the 1980s, I had stomach issues that made me feel

lousy. While turning the pages of a newspaper, I found an article about a Chinese herbal company in Venice, California, that sold herbal tinctures to balance the body and boost the immune system. I had the feeling this was what I needed. I went to the store for more information. A knowledgeable herbalist made some recommendations, and I began to use the products regularly. I was impressed with the results, and within days I started to feel better. I was hooked. The herbs helped relieve my symptoms, and I believed they would help me achieve better health. Within a year I asked the company's founder for a job. I went to work in the offices running promotional campaigns and learning production. The job put me in the center of the action where I could foster my newfound passion for Chinese herbal remedies as an alternative way to improve my health.

I also benefited from the healing philosophies of many interesting people I met at the company. One day the wife of an herbalist was in the Venice store. I told her about a formula I was thinking of trying. She picked up the bottle of herbs and placed her free hand on my arm. She described opening a dialogue with the herbs to determine if they were a good fit for my body. She said, yes, they would be beneficial. She explained her background as a pranic healer. By that time in my life, I was practicing yoga, meditation, and tai chi for strength and mental focus. I was fascinated by the idea of learning new techniques for self-healing.

At home, I would close the shutters in my apartment and

turn off the phone to make the room ready for meditation. Once I had stillness *outside* me, I relaxed until I could feel the stillness *inside* me. From that vantage I would observe the ambient frequency of physical reality—a low background humming I could hear in the silence—and then foster a sense of moving beyond myself. This effort was one of my first inroads to learning about my energetic resources. I was inspired to investigate what I could find on the subject. I had never heard the term "pranic bodywork." While I liked the pranic healer, I was hesitant to let someone work on me because I believed healing should come from within, without any intermediary. Yet the idea of learning from the pranic healer was intriguing.

I scheduled an appointment to discover more. Every week I would lie down on her padded table and the healer's hands would move a few inches above my body without actually touching me. She described the process as removing blockages and opening up energy channels in the system to allow the body to function optimally.

After the appointments, I felt lighter. Perhaps it was psychological because I wanted to feel lighter. She also gave me insights into nutrition and exercise. This information was welcomed as I was always looking to improve my health. Occasionally she gave me feedback on positive or negative influences in my life. One day she started talking about my past lives. I was skeptical on the subject even though throughout my life I had experienced unusual memories I thought were past lives.

I listened to her insights with skepticism. My stance allowed me to be an observer of her process and remain grounded in discernment. In this way I kept my self-exploration active yet separate from the healer's work to have as much clarity as possible. During these sessions, I would interface with a deeper part of myself—what I was beginning to think of as my essence—until I experienced a subtle floating sensation and state of mind that felt like I was moving beyond my body. At the same time, I kept my awareness grounded in my body. Being grounded was imperative. By keeping one foot in the physical world and focusing beyond myself, I could have my awareness in multiple locations to observe my experiences more broadly. My goal was to maintain a clear mind without any pretenses or expectations of the outcome.

One day during a session, an event took place that was so matter-of-fact yet completely stunning in its duration and content. My world was turned on end. The healer told me she could see an object embedded in my head from a past life. I asked her to describe the object. She said, "Some kind of ornate metal headdress." She then said, "You died from responsibility in that lifetime."

I was puzzled and remarked, "People don't die from responsibility." She replied, "You did." At that exact moment I experienced a kind of vision. I was suddenly looking through my eyes into a strangely familiar time and place, standing in another world and witnessing a scene unfolding before me. I was a young man wearing a metal helmet and armor reminiscent of the Middle Ages. I wielded a sword as I fought with another man who was years older, stronger, and a better swordsman. He slashed my shoulder, one of my legs, and finally my torso. I stood back, the wounds consuming me until I dropped to my knees before falling to the ground, bleeding. At that moment, close to death, I looked out at the horizon and saw a field of dead and dying soldiers. I immediately understood I had made decisions leading the soldiers into battle. Most of them died in a brutal fight against a stronger enemy. I could not bear the responsibility of my decision. The emotional toll was overwhelming, an adrenaline surge took over, and I started battling with my fellow soldier. The man was actually my best friend. He reluctantly took my life in self-defense. The vision ended and I was fully present. The healer stood a few feet back, sensing my traumatizing vision. I was winded and stunned. I had never experienced anything like it.

I questioned if the vision was real or if my mind was playing tricks on me. I wondered what forces were at work to generate the scene. Was it a flashback? I tried to shrug it off as a fleeting fantasy of my imagination. That did not work. I was transfixed by the unfolding drama.

I felt an emotional connection to the young man and the circumstances of his death. I began to feel sad and emotionally pained, as if my body knew something my mind did not. Why was I so affected? Was it the death of the soldiers on the field and the events surrounding them, or something else? It was such a clear vision. Where did it come from, and what did it mean?

I tried to assign a source to the vision. I thought, what book or magazine articles did I read? What movie or TV show did I see? Maybe I transposed the story from the influences of media and formed the vision from an unconscious subliminal record. I struggled to place the event in the context of my present life. I could not. I finally found some relief by looking at it from another perspective. I began to treat the vision as a long-forgotten memory I was starting to remember. The shift in my mindset helped me relax and enabled a deeper exploration of my role in what I now know as a past life memory.

I began studying how past life trauma can be carried forward to the present. Past events can remain mostly dormant in the psychological landscape, locked deep within the inner world, thoroughly repressed and unnoticed there. I might have lived lifetimes without too much disturbance from this past material. But the door had been opened, and it helped me understand another layer of sadness, fear, and anger I had been experiencing in my life.

At the time I met the pranic healer at the herbal company, I had been seeking to understand my larger evolution. While my ego may not have been ready for answers, my essence was evidently ready to enlighten me. Little did I know that the vision opened a Pandora's box of implications. The field of dead soldiers was evidence of past pain manifesting in my present circumstances.

I had come to recognize the general unrest and turmoil of inner-world conflicts from my past manifested as symptoms of sadness, anxiety, fear, and anger. Since I can remember, these feelings had remained a potent force, embraced by me as a part of who I had become.

I could easily argue these symptoms resulted from the traumas I experienced at the hands of my biological father. Yet his role merely reflected the conflicts I already possessed. He, too, possessed unresolved conflicts, and the law of attraction put us on a parallel path—two beings of similar energetics coming together to reignite past conflicts on the present stage.

I was further discovering how traumatic events from the past can transfer their discord, remaining present through lifetimes and producing negative emotions. Years later in my early 30s, with the help of my higher self I began to investigate fear and anger and their derivatives. I was learning how the highly charged extreme negative emotions experienced in my past lives—the terror and anger—created fields that linked me to existing fields and remained in the environment. Extreme human emotions have created fear and anger fields throughout a long history of conflict. I had become linked to them like many other people.

Detrimental fear and anger fields are pervasive in our present world. They can only be cleaned up by severing from detrimental fields. During my session with the healer, I unconsciously prompted a psychological mechanism that triggered a long-forgotten memory containing potent ingredients from my past linked to my inner world, influencing the physical, mental, psychological, and spiritual aspects of my being.

First came the insight I had died from responsibility. But without memories to confirm this information, I tried to deny that idea until my vision came, smacking me with the intensity of a fastball. The event of my death from responsibility upended my life and became a catalyst to investigate my inner-world conflicts. To not pull back the layers and look inside would have allowed the obstacles to remain in place with anxiety, sadness, fear, and anger persisting.

I may have been able to hide the emotional energy in the vast landscape of my inner world and keep the trauma out of sight and dormant. But I decided to dive in and learn about the roles and outcomes I created on the battlefields in another time and place. Once I became aware of the pain within me, I had a choice to make. Severing from the source of conflict enabled me to cut ties, close the chapter, and set sights on creating new chapters.

The story of my death from responsibility is another memory from the archives of my history. As I have said, memories are like dust in the wind. They can disperse in the vast inner landscape and inexplicably reconstitute in a visible form. Maybe it was me who had been dispersed like dust in the evolutionary cycles of my existence. The memories coming into alignment in my present world were showing me why I am the way I am. As memories resurfaced, I became empowered to explore myself. The challenge of memories is that they can be forgotten. But what is forgotten can be remembered. I think people look inside themselves for one reason—to see themselves as they are. Their stories are waiting to be discovered. We take what we learn from the past to change ourselves in the present.

Perhaps the healer gave me precisely what I needed. She inspired me to learn from myself. She also reinforced my view that what took place along my journey was not something to be interpreted by an outside party but investigated by me alone. After visiting the healer, I found myself forever changed in how I pursue self-exploration. The benefit any teacher offers their students is the tools to teach themselves. The healer prompted me to open a door and stood back while I entered it. I traveled into another world and came back with the understanding that no one is better suited than I am to take the reins of personal discovery. The resources to conduct research into the history of my spiritual evolution began with a desire to know myself. After my vision of the dead soldiers, I left the healer that day knowing I would never return to her office. That way I could be sure I was as close to the source as possible—myself. To say I was alone in my discoveries would not be entirely accurate. The intelligence and organization of my energetic family in the nonphysical are always with me, assisting me with every step in discovering who I am and why I am. I consider them the only energetically compatible source I allow to be in the driver's seat anytime I venture to explore the larger questions of my evolution. They are uniquely positioned to provide guidance and perspectives for the acquiring of information from other environments. In that capacity, I place no one in higher regard than my energetic system.

The year I met the healer further inspired my curiosity of the Larger Field at play. The healer's role was instrumental in helping me recognize my essence, which became the sounding board to explore existing connections to past lives in worlds beyond. I began moving steadily toward my goal of greater awareness and independence in my spiritual growth. I continued learning about my relationships to other times and places. I discovered my past lifetimes had significant implications in the formation of beliefs that influenced my experiences. Who am I, and why am I the way I am? Each of us arrives at this precise moment in our evolution with a multitude of beliefs. Beliefs play an important role in our lives, for they give us the certainty we thrive on. Many of our beliefs are derived from the world in which we live. But some of our beliefs come with us from other times and places. Our beliefs reflect where we have been and inform where we are going. The following chapters examine the nature of beliefs and the obstacles of trauma, fear, and anger, and their tendency to create fragmentary views of reality which can interfere with our path to wholeness.

FIFTEEN

Crossing the Bridge: A Short Leap to Greater Understanding

Our essence is vastly more extraordinary than our intellect or ego could ever hope to be, beckoning us to know what more there is to experience within the Earth life system and beyond. What I can see is the measure of my reality, and what I adopt as my beliefs are the boundaries I create that set limits upon the stage. When I dream big, I raise the stakes and shatter limits, exposing myself to a union with all that is.

There are many ways we cross the bridge to the nonphysical. A quiet moment to relax can induce tranquility and enable a soft interface with nonphysical environments. Taking a walk in a park, standing in a sunset or under the stars, reading from a book, listening to music, dancing, or playing with a family pet can take us away from the hustle and bustle and shift our attention beyond ourselves. The simple interactions we crave most link us to brighter realms where we may experience our wholeness. The ways the transcendental touches us are endless. Paying attention to everyday interactions builds awareness of the larger reality in our lives.

Many people report the life-changing outcomes from their transcendental experiences—and even if they doubt the validity of brighter realms, they benefit from a powerful sense of fulfillment and purpose. Rarely do people question there is more to reality than can be seen or touched. Some view physical reality as a limited spectrum, in that sensory perception represents only a tiny fraction of reality unfolding beyond them. Others are content to allow transcendental experiences to remain a mystery.

I have known people who deny the existence of spiritual worlds. Yet they find great satisfaction through artistic disciplines or jobs which require immense organization and intelligence as they unconsciously reach for existing connections beyond themselves and experience the colorful strata of their personal evolution.

For others, the worlds beyond are explored through practices and belief systems to discover meaning through spiritual attainment and enlightenment. Some suggest the pursuit of spiritual knowledge is to transcend the confinement of physical life and free the spirit. My nonphysical counterparts suggest we have the unique opportunity to integrate the full energetic capability of our system while living in the physical environment.

Some people believe physical reality is an illusion, while others believe reality is an impressive creation. According to my system, reality is agreed intent. To merge with the nonphysical while remaining in a physical body means we have the inheritance of access. Whether we acknowledge the nonphysical in our lives or not, we are members of the human race representing our energetic origin. Physicality gives us the stage to play unique parts. As actors, we are responsible for the roles we create, defined by our intellect, personality, ego, emotions, actions, and of course our intention. From a purely energetic point of view, people are inexorably linked together with striking similarities. We are all energetic beings—however, our destinies take us in vastly different directions from each other. The differences are as diverse as the many beliefs and perceptions we adopt along the way. Beliefs have a powerful influence on our experiences in the physical world.

We thrive on the certainty of our beliefs and give them power as they represent the assurance of stability. Beliefs also represent ideas and viewpoints accepted without validation. I may accept the idea that trees are made of wood, but that idea is still a belief I have willingly adopted. Consensus beliefs on physical reality—what it looks like and how it operates, with gravity, air, Earth, and space—provide us the orientation we rely on to make sense of our world as we know it. When we agree on our observations, our expectations align and we're on the same page. Mass agreement on physical reality gives us a common ground to share our experiences. However other beliefs do not fall under the general rule of consensus beliefs.

Conceptual beliefs have a very different role in the human world. Many stories and mythologies throughout human history reflect a vivid array of conceptual belief systems that tell stories of the interconnected nature of the physical and spiritual worlds. We adopt the stories as metaphors that inspire us to seek further understanding of our relationships with each other and worlds beyond us. The idea of the Larger Field is subjective. So is the nonphysical. We have a choice in how we interpret our beliefs. But whatever we believe is inconsequential to the experience all people have in common. We live and die. We experience loneliness. We thrive on human affection and love. The fundamental reality of physical life is unchanged by our beliefs.

We look into a mirror and recognize we are more than our body. The insights from this simple idea elevate the transcendental in our lives as a thematic underpinning of human experience, no matter where we come from or what we believe. We have split off from our nonphysical energetic family to experience our particular galactic space, where time unfolds in a high-density planetary environment defined by boundaries known as the physical universe. Exploring spiritual worlds requires us to suspend our limiting perceptions and reach beyond ourselves to experience who, what, and why we are. However, the ability to experience our energetic legacy has mostly been forgotten in human civilization. What is forgotten can be remembered.

My spiritual mentor said, "We don't become anything because we already are, yet we always create." This simple message suggests we exist beyond our present world. Our existence is without end, and we are the seat of creation. We think and create. That's what we do in every interaction, every day. I added to my mentor's thought—it's what we create that demands our attention and responsibility. Human beings are like creation machines. We think with intention and create outcomes. That is our main role in the physical world. What we create in physicality happens precisely because we are informed by the worlds we come from before life. Indeed, we merge the nonphysical and physical resources to manifest the world we live in.

The Earth existed before we came along, but the foundation of human civilization is a joint endeavor between people and their nonphysical counterparts. We may think we're alone. Yet our roles as creators are supported by existing connections to our energy system—our nonphysical core family. From their unique vantage, we are seen as actors playing a part on a vast creative stage. Each of our creations is an opportunity to open vistas to yet countless other worlds.

We humans have absorbed many kinds of beliefs from birth—consensus beliefs—with mass agreement on physical reality and conceptual beliefs, where human differences are expressed through ideologies, religions, ethnicities, dogmas, national identities, etc. As members of the human race, we have a lot of experience with our beliefs.

During my lifetime, I have embraced many different beliefs that significantly influenced how I lived. The framing of beliefs starts when we discover our independence in childhood. Some beliefs are extremely useful and even necessary for living in the physical world, while others are not. When I was younger, I was more likely to believe what others believed without validation. I had not learned to exercise discernment about which beliefs were useful and which were unnecessary.

If someone told me I could see the stars in the Milky Way, I had no reason not to believe that idea. Eventually I learned of scientific studies proving that stars generated their light millions of years ago. Thus, I see the light of the stars, not the actual stars. This view of the physical universe transformed my outlook. I began to understand how the beliefs I adopt significantly influence my reality. The world is constantly changing, and with it my views, beliefs, and perceptions are transformed as new sources of information become available. This example of consensus beliefs relates to mass agreement on physical reality. But conceptual beliefs can also have a significant impact on how reality is interpreted and experienced. What is a conceptual belief? Something that cannot be validated through knowledge alone. Something of which people don't have experiential evidence. Something that someone else asked us to agree with. Something approved by society but not by individual experience.

The story of my mother losing her father and hearing his voice conjures ideas that can easily be interpreted in the realm of belief. Others might say she manifested a psychological mechanism to help her let go and move on. My mother might even agree with that hypothesis. She felt strongly about proof and validation, but the event gave her a powerful feeling of resolve and peace. Sensing her father was not far away freed her from grief and anguish. Some might have accepted she had a bona fide transcendental experience and a communication from the nonphysical.

Years later, she felt her mother close by when she died. She understood that the bonds she cherished most were alive and well. My mother achieved a transcendental awareness, knowing she was not far away from the people she loved. Her understanding was individually obtained through direct, personal association with the Larger Field—that is, from contact with sources of information outside of sensory, intellectual, mental, and technological processes. She learned to set herself free in brighter realms.

Beliefs in the human world take many forms. In my 20s I was invited to attend a meeting led by a guru who came to the city to meet his followers. As a spiritual leader, he spoke in depth about spiritual attainment. He talked about how he had evolved his being by practicing meditation and living with holy cave people, whose food he described as being the most empowering food he had ever eaten because it was made from the pure love of the holy people. He carried on about how remarkable and energizing the food made him feel. I objected to his message. I felt he was self-aggrandizing as he suggested that none of his followers could experience food made with the pure love of holy people. Holiness can be found in a mother or father's heart or a child's spirit. Unbounded devotion, love, and compassion is holy unto itself. Most people know the experience of food made with love. Calmly but defiantly, I interjected, "Your story reminds me of the high holidays when my grandmothers served empowering food made with all the love in their being." The guru's calm demeanor turned agitated. He stared at me with a cold gaze, his manner unwelcoming of my sentiments as he continued speaking. I felt alienated but wasn't terribly surprised at his reaction. The guru missed an opportunity to address a subject most people could relate to and a lesson that could have been taught. As he carried on my instincts told me he was unable to speak humbly to his audience. I went to the guru expecting to learn something about myself and feel inspired, but instead I encountered a spiritual man who was not a unifying figure.

Later that year I became friends with a rabbi who invited me to Shabbat dinner at his home over a period of months. He spoke openly of forgiveness and inclusion of all people no matter their background. At the time, I was representing a German artist who was traveling to Los Angeles and needed a place to stay. The rabbi offered her one of the apartments he used for out-of-town guests. When she arrived to meet the rabbi he noted her distinct European accent and asked about her birth city. She replied, "Berlin."

During the night as she slept, the rabbi came to her window and began to repeat in a low, eerie tone, "You burned us in the ovens." She was awakened, thinking she was having a nightmare. When she realized it was the rabbi at the window, she quickly dressed, packed up, and ran out into the cold night.

The rabbi was unable to accept her. His beliefs precluded his ability to see past the anger that permeated his being over the injustices of the Holocaust. While he did not experience the atrocities of World War II firsthand, he was influenced by the collective trauma that impacted many people around the world. He adopted a belief system of anger and distrust. His beliefs created a fragmentary mindset which reflected his outlook. Forgiveness and inclusion may have been in his mind, but not his heart.

Throughout the world are countless examples of the breakdown of unification between people, societies, and nations. Me from you, us from them, my belief from your belief. Fragmentation serves to divide us from the undivided wholeness of ourselves. Conceptual beliefs tend to represent inflexible attitudes and judgments which often provoke extreme prejudice. Unwarranted fears and anger are unstable factors that can profoundly influence societies. Fragmentation is a symptom of humankind's separation from the Larger Field and disconnection from the higher self. Fragmentation is a fundamental function of humankind's long night of ignorance. In the Larger Field fragmentation does not exist. Divisiveness and separation only exist in human societies. People create them. Separation leads to a fragmentary mindset which perpetuates the dilemma we face.

Human belief structures have led to a dark and fragmentary view of reality. In our blindness, many act like a single individual adrift on a raft in the middle of a vast empty ocean. In the nonphysical, there is no separation. We are connected to one another. On the planet Earth most people do not see. Some do see. More are starting to operate in a linked fashion.

SIXTEEN

A New Father: The Bonds That Matter

What I know is what I can experience, and the prevailing influence behind my experience is what I intend to create in the Larger Field. When we leave our intellect and ego at the door and place our attention inward, we can learn to sense our essence, giving us the advantage of greater self-awareness. From there, all roads lead to our higher self and energetic system. From the top down, the higher self has sent an extension of itself into physicality—that is us—through the extension's temporary presence as a human being, also us. Our essence is only a fraction, a portion of the higher self that is infinitely more massive than us. Thus, we become the connective tissue between worlds and return someday to our higher self with our life experiences. But while in the physical world, it's important to know our experiences—for good or bad—are just moments in time in a temporary realm that can lift us to wonderous heights or bog us down with the weight of emotions. Our essence is unconstrained by this weight, for its role represents the boundlessness of what and who we are. It's ironic that during our lives we collect evidence of our boundless nature, yet we might hardly recognize the insights we gain as valid or important. Indeed, the glimpses are reflections of our true energetic nature, and when we start paying attention, we open doors in the Larger Field.

Whether or not people recognize the transcendental in their lives is irrelevant to the role of the Larger Field permeating human interactions with intuition, insight, and understanding of ourselves. Crossing paths with people with whom we recognize a deeper connection can be liberating. Relationships become ever more fascinating when destinies align and brighter realms inspire our journey.

We might discover deeper bonds. Relationships take on new meaning as we find our likeness, even with the most unlikely people. We might not be able to voice the mysterious sense of connection we feel, yet the familiarity is undeniable. Discovering our transcendental nature reveals wondrous clarity, forever changing our lives in the unbounded playfulness of the universe. While I know people who recognize the existence of other worlds, I also know people who resist the idea of worlds beyond themselves. They maintain limits to what they are willing to accept, and with good reason.

My mother's beliefs were influenced by her upbringing, the

values she adopted from her parents, school, and her religious experiences. As a young girl she was told by her pastor there were angels in the clouds. When she searched the clouds in her father's airplane, she did not see angels. But her pastor insisted they were there although she was unable to see them.

She put her beliefs aside and decided to question what she could not validate through direct experience, the physical senses, intellect, logic, and reason. Regardless of her standards, she came to terms with the passing of her parents by accepting that the bonds between them were alive and well. When I was five years old my mother introduced my brother, sisters, and me to a man she was falling in love with. He happened to be uniquely close to his energy system. When they started dating, she got cold feet and told him she wasn't ready for a relationship. She had come from a broken marriage. I was three years old when she kicked my biological father out of our home. She was understandably proceeding cautiously with a new relationship.

Months passed and she had a change of heart, an intuition that the man was good. She called and asked for a rain check. It wasn't long before they started dating again. I can still remember the little boxes filled with black-and-white curly cue licorice that would bring smiles and delight to my siblings and me. We saw my mother was happy with him. The day they told us they would be married I asked one question: "Does that mean he will have dinner with us every night?" Our destinies aligned, and we never looked back. Our parents united and we were a whole family again. It was a courageous leap for a single mother of four young children and a confirmed bachelor. Their union was perfect synchronicity, and it led to 55 years of love. One day our new father took us to meet his parents, our new grandparents. At their home he was excited to show us a ceramic jar on the entry table full of dried roses from his parent's wedding day in 1921. The family huddled as my new grandmother lifted the top off the jar. When it was my turn to look inside, my senses flooded with pure fragrance as if the roses had just been placed inside the jar. The roses became my ritual when visiting my grandparents. I'd gently remove the top, leaning over the jar to take in the captivating aromas, stir the petals with my fingers, and find myself carried away to another world.

Ten years later my mother picked me up from school with tears in her eyes and news of my grandmother's passing. After the funeral I was standing alone near the jar of roses at my aunt and uncle's house. My grandfather quietly walked to the table, clasped his hands on the jar, and said, "Roses of love for fifty-seven years." At that moment, I began to understand that death is not a loss of bonds but a continuation of them. At 15 years of age his grieving made a big impression on me. I watched my grandfather far away from his usual self in an intimate communication with another world. Yet he was the most present person in the house.

Decades later, the feeling returned when my mother passed

away. My father, sisters, brother, and I stood at her bedside. As she lay dying, we found ourselves converging at the edge of the world she was moving toward, and for brief moments we glimpsed that world and showed our acceptance of her departure into it. When the time came a warm sensation filled my body and gently subsided as she brushed by me on her way. I felt her with every cell in my body, and I knew her move was complete. No lingering part of her remained.

Death says we cease. Yet I never felt any disconnection from her, our bond remaining unchanged. She died as she had lived, with decision and action. She had the unique quality to always be herself. For 60 years she was the unifying figure in my life, showing me that real strength comes from the core, essence, and soul of a human being. Undeniably, what is unseen when glancing into a mirror is widely present throughout life and most visibly evidenced in death. The closure of a chapter opened a new phase uniting me with eternal bonds to brighter realms like those who came and left before her. For now, when I miss her, I am reminded of the roses from my grandparent's home—as timeless and enduring as the story of her life. My mother helped many people during her lifetime. She was active in charities and worked as a court advocate in Southeast Los Angeles to help displaced children find caring homes. I have very fond memories of my childhood—her love and nurturing were the stabilizing force in my life. A friend once asked me who her favorite child was among my sisters and brother. I replied, "We were all her favorite." I always felt she gave herself fully to our welfare and happiness. She treated all people with equanimity. Her honesty was selfless and considerate. She made you feel special because she was present in her love of life.

She told me the birth of my siblings and I made her happier than she thought possible. The woman I knew as my mother continues. Bonds represent our connections to people present and past, existing without limits or boundaries. The commencement of bonds takes place with the intention to form agreements.

The agreements we form with people during our physical lives have energetic implications linking us to the nonphysical. Our legacy is not only what we leave in the world. We may die and close the chapter of life, but our bonds continue to unify us between the physical and nonphysical.

Ultimately, we are mutual participants in the creation of our bonds. We choose them. They choose us. My mother, siblings and I immediately bonded with our new father, as our union was a synchronicity. Our agreements reflected what was meant to be through our bonds. The nature of our bonds exists beyond our beliefs, for they need no validation by a belief system, yet beliefs may play a role in creating our bonds. Generally speaking, we know how we feel about people. We know when we care or feel empathy, compassion, and love. What is known represents transcendental connections linking us to each other. Knowing reflects our unbounded intuition by merging us with the clarity of brighter realms. Knowing links us to our nonphysical origin. But these links can become compromised for any number of reasons, including trauma, which creates obstacles to our higher self and energetic family. I am no stranger to the many obstacles I've encountered during my life. I have had my share of trauma, the complications of which have taken me on a path far away from my higher self, yet eventually giving me the understanding to find my way to wholeness.

SEVENTEEN

The Fear and Anger Inside Us: Losing Sight of Ourselves

Our agreements can link us to detrimental encounters where fear and anger form a collective field of negativity. Unfortunately, we live in a world where fear and anger represent a pervasive theme, creating fragmentary worldviews that make it difficult to experience a connection to our essence and the positive resources of caring, empathy, compassion, and love. Being displaced from our energetic counterparts means we can miss out on the larger story of our essence interacting in brighter realms.

Many of the events I write about in this book took place before I clearly understood the nonphysical's role in my life. My gut feelings, intuitions, insights, and past memories were signs of my access to nonphysical resources, giving me a view ahead. But there have been periods during my history where I became submerged in fear or anger and experienced the depths of emotional pain. The extreme emotional states could disconnect me from my nonphysical counterparts or, conversely, provide the awareness to establish connection and rise above fear or anger. The ways people rise above adversity in their lives are countless—the unconscious connections with nonphysical resources present a foundation of strength that, no matter the perils people go through, can remain relatively untouched, even in extreme circumstances. Nonphysical connection can mean protection. The nonphysical can also be a double-edged sword. The experience of trauma is an example of nonphysical interaction having detrimental, life-changing implications. Extreme emotional conflicts can induce trauma. Some people can remain unharmed, free of the negative fear or anger fields associated with trauma. Their experience is as an observer and not a participant. Fear or anger can also be overwhelming, impacting a human being with lasting trauma as an external field linked to and embedded internally within a person's inner world.

What are fear and anger fields? People are not only creation machines manifesting the world we live in. We also manifest our thoughts as energetic fields. Thoughts are the inception of our potential to create. Thought energy is also the result of the feelings and emotions we manifest. Have you ever met someone who felt happy or sad? You might sense their state of mind if you're tuned in. What about fear or anger? Negative emotions are usually easier to feel. They are also at the root of human potential to create a negative implication, for the extreme states of mind relating to fear and anger can result in high output energy generated by human thoughts, leaving residual detrimental fields in the physical environment.

Our thoughts have significant implications for our world, whether we create with beneficial or nonbeneficial intent. However, negative fields exist because humans create them when extreme fear or anger comes into play. When a person experiences a traumatic event, they can inadvertently link to existing fear or anger fields. The ways trauma can inflict a person are manifold.

When my mother was 13 years old, she was assaulted by two men who tried to grab her as she walked in her school hallway. I asked how she got away. She replied, "I fought hard, broke free and ran for my life." While her life was dominated by kindness, caring, and love, the traumatic experience left her with pain.

For the rest of her life, she would occasionally experience fearful emotions around the memory. My mother had become linked to nonphysical fear fields, causing an emotional flashback. She had a strong psychological constitution which enabled her to compartmentalize the fear fields within her inner world and keep the negative energy mostly dormant and out of sight. Yet occasionally, the fear could cause her anguish. Many people experience traumas with varying effects lasting a lifetime.

I have a friend who, as a child, witnessed her parents'

recurring fights over money. Hiding behind walls, she felt helpless and frightened. Without any way to retreat, she wished they would get divorced. The overwhelming events caused her to experience heightened anxiety and excessive fear, resulting in trauma.

On weekends the family would go to the ice cream parlor, where everyone would pick their favorite flavor. While her siblings gleefully started eating their scoops of ice cream, my friend would wait, fearful she'd have to give her scoop back if her father couldn't pay. Once she heard the register ring up, she felt relieved and could start eating.

In later years she developed attachments to material items, books, accessories, clothing, shoes—anything of value she acquired with money provoked anxious feelings, causing her inability to let go of the stuff years after it was no longer useful.

When she attempted to divest herself, she was returned to the overwhelming emotions, as trauma dysregulated her with painful emotional flashbacks from her childhood shame concerning money. The memory loop of old emotions ran her life. She worked hard to make money, becoming successful in her career but held onto a deep-seated fear of being unable to afford her basic living needs. The irony is that her parents had enough money to raise their family. It was her father who had a psychological weakness. He had survived World War II and suffered post-traumatic stress disorder. He was a loving father, but he could erupt at the slightest change in his environment, experiencing emotional collapse when dealing with ordinary stress. His inability to cope led him to instigate fights with his wife and inadvertently involve their children in his pervasive trauma, causing his family to interface with the fear and anger fields linked to his inner world.

For a child, a loud, angry voice can induce trauma. My friend eventually learned to identify the origin of her trauma and the symptoms of dysregulation. She became aware that trauma can be transferable between people. While she was not responsible for her father's trauma, she learned to accept her role in the manifestation of trauma and its implications in her life. The trauma wasn't her fault, but it was her responsibility to heal herself. When she gained insight into her trauma, she was able to find resolve and open new pathways for the future.

Animals can also experience trauma. I once met a puppy who feared his own front yard. The owners would open the front door to go for a walk, but the puppy would panic and resist going outside. The family got into the habit of picking up the puppy and carrying it to the sidewalk. Once at the sidewalk, the puppy was okay for a walk through the neighborhood. When the family returned home, the puppy panicked again upon entering the front yard. The family revealed the inciting incident. The puppy was playing in the front yard when an older dog entered the yard with a neighbor. The puppy playfully jumped at the older dog. The older dog asserted its dominance and snapped back at the puppy to correct its behavior. The older dog was teaching the puppy how to behave. But a family member swooped the puppy up, holding it with fear and panic, screaming at the older dog to get back. From that moment, the puppy was traumatized—not by the older dog, but by the human who displayed an intense emotional fear reaction, transferring and linking the puppy to an energetic fear field. I suggested they make the front yard a fun and happy place for the puppy by gradually introducing treats, and mealtimes there. Eventually, the puppy was able to overcome its fear of the front yard. Unfortunately, some traumas can become far more embedded within the inner world.

Dutch Shepherds are heroic dogs popular with police and the military. These dogs are known to be fearless in the field and able to adapt to extreme conditions. They can become injured and continue their mission to completion. The handler of a Dutch Shepherd builds attention with consistent praise and reward. In turn, the dogs become devoted protectors of their human counterparts.

There is only one problem—if the handler gets into a life-threatening situation and suffers trauma, their dog can become linked to fear fields generated by their connection to the handler. If the handler experiences trauma, the dogs can also experience trauma. In extreme cases, the dogs cannot be rehabilitated from severe handler-related trauma and must return to civilian life.

Many years ago, I met a woman who escaped from Germany

during the outset of World War II. As a child she went into hiding in the small village where she lived. A group of partisans came to help her and others from the village escape the country. There was only one requirement of the escape group—they must not make a sound. The children could not cry or show emotion or they would be caught and killed. During daylight hours the group hid in forests and fields. They moved only at night, eventually escaping across the border to safety. After the event, the woman discovered she had lost her ability to cry or get in touch with her emotions. Traumatized by the event that left her emotionally disabled, her natural reactions were no longer accessible. Nonphysical energetic fear fields triggered stifling interference and compromised her ability to experience normal emotions.

I grew up with a friend who came from a broken home. Her parents never got along. They fought each other with contempt and disrespect. The negative emotions overflowed in the home, placing the children in the crosshairs of anger fields. As the children grew older, they could either participate in the contemptuous behaviors introduced by their parents or remain outside the conflicts. My friend chose to stay out of the detrimental anger fields. From a young age, her instincts helped her avoid the strife at home. She learned to protect herself and even disarm her parents because she was not receptive to their conflicts. It was as if she could surround herself with a shield of feathers—waterproof against the anger and strife. At the same time, she could reciprocate her parents' negativity with caring, empathy, and love.

Her siblings did not fare as well. They took on the anger fields and contributed to the conflicts. My friend's ability to remain neutral gave her a great advantage in personal relationships. She grew up, left her parents' home, and was able to lead a well-balanced and happy life. Those qualities benefited her because of her inherent connections to inner resources of a nonphysical origin.

My friend is an example of an individual functioning according to principles acquired from her energetic core family. She may not have recognized the nonphysical's role in her life, yet she worked in accordance with the nonphysical just the same. The stories in this chapter illustrate how nonphysical fear and anger fields can affect life. Recognizing the potential impact of the environment in which we live can give us a clear advantage for adaptation. Our world constantly tests us, challenging our resolve to avoid conflicts or join them. We can become impacted by circumstances beyond our control and, with the support of our system, work toward resolve and healing.

EIGHTEEN

The Twin Towers: When Fear Takes Over

When we live without connection to our essence, we are effectively displaced from our energy system and can become vulnerable to the plight of evil. The ways evil manifests in people can only be dealt with by looking beyond ourselves to the origin of fear and anger. To understand how we participate with fear and anger can give us the stance to gently but firmly reject its role in our life. Learning about the fundamental stuff we are made of—energy—provides us with a broader context to see things as they are. Everything physical and nonphysical is thought energy.

The phone rang in the morning of September 11, 2001. My mother urgently told me the country was under attack. As I turned on the TV and saw the unfolding tragedy, I knew I would have to make a decision. I could either submerge myself in fear and anger or remain outside the weight of my emotions.

I chose the latter. I desperately wanted to understand what was happening on the energetic level, to see the bigger picture and not become swept away by the terror like so many people. I hoped being objective might give me the advantage to be useful and assist others in the uncertain days ahead. While the towers were burning, people across the nation went home to be with their families. Airspace was cleared. Fire departments were mobilized and military aircraft took to the skies. As the country braced itself against more attacks, an eerie silence settled over the nation.

I immediately called family and friends. I could feel a great deal of emotion in their voices, their shock manifesting as the day went on. I could detect fear and anger in every person with whom I spoke. It was challenging not to participate in the crush of emotions I felt around me, although I made an effort to remain outside the conflict. I would not allow myself to be submerged in what I perceived as the fields of fear and anger that can link people to a collective field of detrimental energy and, once linked, be all-consuming and indefinite.

Forming intention out of fear and anger can produce a disconnection from the energetic core family, creating vulnerabilities to the existing fear and anger fields, leading to destructive outcomes. Not linking with fear and anger fields means remaining independent and free of their influence.

I tried to center myself, to push my emotions aside and remain as neutral as possible. I focused my mind on not participating in the collective negativity. By that afternoon I made the rounds, driving across town to visit family and friends.

I met with an old friend who I had known to be a peaceful and easy-going guy. He acted in films, wrote screenplays, and played jazz on his piano. He always had a positive outlook—the kind of person who consistently saw the brighter side of life. On this day, however, the person I had known for years was not present. He was quiet and withdrawn, his skin looked flush, and his expression sullen. We sat in his living room with an awkward silence. My friend was hardly present.

I finally spoke and shared the idea that the people crashing the planes into the towers had lost their souls to commit such a heinous act. He looked at me coldly and replied, "We should drop a bomb."

I replied, "Who do you want to kill?"

"I don't know," he quipped. He repeated, "We should drop a bomb."

I replied, "Be careful what you think and say, there can be consequences." He just shook his head, saying, "I don't care. We should drop a bomb."

I realized my friend could not see beyond the fear and anger he was creating. I also understood he had become inadvertently linked to existing fear and anger fields.

He wanted only one thing—revenge on the perpetrators—and he wasn't the only person who believed this was what needed to be done. Later that day I spoke with another friend who told me he could see himself in Army fatigues going after the terrorists and killing them one by one. I tried to empathize with my friend's feelings, yet I felt awkward because I did not share his anger. I could not put myself in his shoes because I made an agreement with myself to remain outside the influence of fear and anger and not become swept away. My friends were unconsciously pulled into the pervasively dark theme that took hold of people the day the towers fell.

I warned my friends of the consequences of contributing to the pervasive fear and anger fields created by millions across the nation. My reasoning fell on deaf ears. In another conversation, I spoke with a friend who was visiting a Middle Eastern country at the time of the attacks. He told me that the moment the news came of the towers' destruction, people took to the streets in celebrations that lasted for days. I was shocked. An eerie disbelief came over me, similar to the moments the planes crashed into the towers.

Later that afternoon I began journaling about the events of the day. I wrote about the loss of innocent lives. I wrote about evil manifesting in human beings. I wrote about terrorists displaced from their souls, committing heinous acts of terror and destruction. I also wrote about my desire to remain free of the fear and anger generated by millions of people across the planet. And I wrote about the hatred that would motivate a human being to celebrate the death of other human beings. I wrote about the highly charged emotional state that immersed my friends in fear and anger and how such energy could replicate itself and create more destructive events.

After a year had passed, the world was on the verge of a second Gulf War. Days before the war began, I visited my friend who had said he wanted to drop a bomb. We sat in the same room on the same chairs where we had met after the 911 attack. I was pleasantly surprised by his peaceful course reversal. He told me he was not happy about the prospect of war. I was glad to hear he had a change of heart.

He said, "I don't want this war. Do you want this war? Nobody wants this war."

At that point, I cut him off and said, "Wait a minute, this is your war. You created this war." He looked at me, puzzled. I continued, "After the towers fell, you were out for blood." I reminded him of the exact words he said about dropping a bomb, "Now your thoughts, and the thoughts of millions more, who manifested anger and hatred and urged retaliation are coming true." I told my friend the coming war is the result of these collective thoughts. I asserted, "You're going to get your bomb in all-out warfare."

He looked into my eyes and replied, "I never said that."

I reminded him of his single-minded intention about dropping a bomb on the day the towers fell. Again, he denied having ever been in the state of mind to speak those words. I then told him I went home that day and wrote down his thoughts, word for word.

We had different positions on the events of that day. In the scheme of things, he had a change of heart, which was good for him. Weeks later I told the story to a psychologist friend who explained denial was a common theme among her patients. In the case of my friend, the fear and anger that swept him away were hidden even from himself. My psychologist friend suggested that until we learn to face our shadows we will continue to struggle with our conflicts. Everything we create begins with a thought. Our thoughts have extraordinary power to create progress, or they can have a detrimental effect.

People are the casualties of pervasive fear and anger fields, creating a theme of fragmentation, seeing only the differences between me and you, us from them, separated, divided, isolated, and susceptible to becoming influenced by ideologies and dogmas that can foster destruction. Fragmentary worldviews separate human beings from their fundamental wholeness. This is the conflict between light and dark. The essential elements to wholeness can be recovered, but it means people must resolve to accept who they will become when fear and anger are no longer present.

The day the towers fell, I had become an inadvertent observer of the perverse and irrational underpinnings of terror unfolding on humanity's grand stage. I wondered why I came to a world that permits such acts to decimate what people hold of the highest value: life. Fear and anger exist because people create them, and the collective thoughts of humanity has the power to sustain them.

Human beings are creation machines. We create the societal structures and physical infrastructures we live in. From thoughts and ideas, we create growth or destruction. All people contribute to the world, for good or bad. We are actors playing a unique part on the vast creative stage, except our emotions and thoughts have the power to modify and alter our world in terrible and fantastic ways. Like many others, I have had a long history in the Earth life system. Through thought and action, I have participated and contributed to the theme of warfare during my evolution. I have also changed the course of my spiritual evolution by choosing to realign my intentions to be a builder rather than a destroyer.

By recognizing my essence and higher self, I have discovered freedom and independence of spirit, giving my life to the advancement of humanity. Those who choose to move forward with their spiritual evolution have the potential to rebuild the crucial links to their nonphysical counterparts. Becoming aware of our capability for wholeness is the first step to building a bridge between our essence and our nonphysical identity, creating the opportunity for peace to be discovered in brighter realms.

NINETEEN

Changes: How Awareness Transforms

It's up to us to make the world a better place. Taking action is too often circumvented by fear. We worry about solutions to the problems we face. But problems drive progress. The capacity to solve problems begins with the awareness of ourselves and by envisioning the future we want to create. The opportunity to shape the future lies in our hands. I like the saying, "Be the change you want to see in the world." This simple idea upholds the highest value—when we make constructive contributions to our lives, we contribute to the world. This positive statement reflects the benefit we offer the world by immersing our best selves in life. In so doing we influence the course of human evolution.

To be born human is to be subject to the one certainty no one escapes: change. There were years when I took notice of changes in the world around me, but not in my own life. In my teens I used to think changes in my life were about learning new skills, getting a job to make money, or meeting new friends. I worked out and rode my 10-speed on long rides to improve my fitness. These endeavors were important to making positive changes in my life. I improved myself because it felt good and right. I also changed myself to fit the expectations of society.

Like many of us who want to fit into the mainstream, I sought change outside me, unaware of the real changes unfolding inside me on an energetic level. Ironically, I barely recognized the most important changes that were happening to me. I had transcendental experiences since childhood and, for many years, did not consider these wondrous events to be worthy of exploration. The events happened so frequently they appeared trivial to me. Occasionally, when I attempted to tell friends and family they turned away with a worried expression.

I understood why people could not relate to my stories. My experiences were not aligned with the world's expectations. Through the years I would revisit my unusual experiences and try to understand what they meant. In adulthood, I began journaling daily. I wrote with such frequency and duration, I discovered the stories represented who, what, and why I am.

I often wonder how different the world would be if people's transcendental experiences were met with open minds where intuition was praised with support to look beyond ourselves. Where societies recognize the significance of personal exploration and discovery of other worlds beyond. Someday I am certain we will live in a world that outwardly roots for the spiritual evolution of all humanity. I was fortunate to have a supportive family who nurtured my emotional well-being and encouraged independence and freedom of thought.

But children learn to express the innate qualities of their essence, endowed by their nonphysical counterparts and reciprocated by their family members. There is little question that many children are born predisposed to extraordinary values which come with them from their nonphysical origin. For each of us, the physical world is the stage to express what already exists within us. The inherent virtues of our essence represent our wholeness unified by the worlds we come from. Learning to share our inherent qualities freely is our first rehearsal of the transcendental unfolding in our lives. Kindness and caring are our contributions informed by our energetic counterparts.

To see the world through the lens of nonphysical understanding is the most important contributing factor to seeing ourselves and others as we are—partly physical and nonphysical beings born to experience the physical world. Whether we know it or not, our lives make us participants in the transcendental legacy of humanity. From a young age, I tried to understand why family and friends did not experience the transcendental as I did. I struggled to fit into the world on my terms. So, I made an effort to meet the world on its terms.

I attended religious services with my family. I would spend the holidays participating in observances with altars, rituals, and ceremonies meant to bridge the physical and spiritual worlds. Although the belief structures I grew up with did not reflect my personal experiences, I liked the stories of ancient peoples adopting the values of love, compassion, tolerance, and forgiveness, instilling meaning and encouraging unification in the present.

For years I never considered other worlds, evidenced in my transcendental experiences, as offering values I could learn from. In fact, the core human values were already inherent within me, as they are within many people. Eventually, my experiences gave me a starting point to understand myself. During my 20s I studied different belief systems and found myself feeling uncertain about my role in the world. I felt stuck, unable to move ahead, but in actuality there were many changes taking place inside of me. I got married and set a course for a new chapter as I searched for greater meaning and fulfillment.

At 23, I lived along the "Borscht Belt" in the Jewish Quarter of Los Angeles. I interacted daily with the local Orthodox and Hasidic Jews and became friends with a Kabbalah scholar who invited me to a study group. I struck up a close friendship with an Orthodox Jewish student who was my age. We shared remarkably similar views and spoke for hours about the interconnected nature of the physical and spiritual worlds.

Our relationship abruptly ended, however, when the local rabbi forbade contact with each other. I was an outsider, and the rabbi thought our belief systems were incompatible. I grew disillusioned with a belief system that would separate people when its core message encouraged unification between spiritual and human worlds.

The ending of our friendship motivated me to understand the divide between us. My comparative study took a turn as I began investigating the origin of belief systems. Where did they come from? What was the purpose of these systems? Under the guidance of my mentor, I delved into the diverse roles that belief systems play worldwide. I concluded that the core of most belief systems offers a nearly parallel message of love, caring, compassion, and unification to help people build meaningful relationships and meet the challenges of the physical environment.

Belief systems have the potential to unite people from all walks of life. Yet, the result of many different beliefs among humans also has the side effect of divisiveness, creating separation between people and societies. I wanted to know why. My quest for understanding led me to a simple yet profound realization of human interpretation. Nonphysical systems, including the higher self, have communicated with their human counterparts since the beginning of time. However, the knowledge from oral communications was passed down generationally and transcribed over the millennium, with each generation adding its interpretations, thus altering the original intent of the information. Geography, culture, and subjective handling have played a significant role influencing belief systems.

The altering of nonphysical information is a common theme throughout human history, resulting in the formation of many different beliefs disseminated, adopted, and organized by humans. This has had a splintering effect on societies and a breakdown of unification among people. Fragmentary worldviews have interrupted the natural ability of people to link with their nonphysical counterparts. Information from the nonphysical once offered an essential bridge to wholeness. Human interpretation compromised the unification of people with their energetic origin.

I moved to Colorado and spent my free time meditating in nature and studying at the Naropa Institute Library to learn about different philosophies, religions, and spiritual systems. The library fed my desire to explore the nature of reality. I journaled extensively to gain better self-awareness. I was looking for an internal access hatch to pursue the transcendental deliberately, to gain understanding and comprehension of my relationship to life and worlds beyond me.

I was searching for answers but found only questions. My path eventually led me to my mentor who helped me uncover the voice I had been hearing in the back of my mind since childhood. That voice was trying to show me a path to new understanding. Little did I know the steps I was about to take would introduce the clarity I longed for.

TWENTY

The Nonphysical: Making Contact

There will always be moments when we make critical decisions about the rest of our lives. Our choices may seem ordinary and uneventful, yet unbeknownst to us we have crossed a threshold from which our lives will never be the same. To embrace this idea is to step aside from our ego and allow our essence into the forefront of the journey, to lead us across the once invisible spaces where dreams intersect reality and agreements made in the brighter realms reveal our greatest purpose. As we learn to get ourselves out of the way, we make room for profound growth.

In 1994, I stepped into the office of a man who was teaching a unique process to access the nonphysical and one's energetic family. He had a degree in philosophy, spoke multiple languages, and reminded me of a university professor with a classic beard, sports jacket, and button-down shirt. What captured my attention was his fascinating grasp of the dynamics of self-discovery. After our first meeting, I decided I wanted to learn from him. He described methods to access the nonphysical and I realized I could explore many of my questions through the proposed work. He would become my mentor. With his guidance I took my first steps to explore the nonphysical realm and discover my energetic self. Once a week after work I made a 50-minute trip to Denver to see him. During each visit we would spend time in a philosophical discussion on various subjects I had been curious about since my childhood.

I was on a path to assimilate my lifetime of transcendental experiences into a cohesive understanding of my relationship with other worlds. The framework of the study was learning to conduct my explorations without a third-party interpretation, meaning I could learn from myself. My mentor provided the tools for me and then got out of the way, allowing me to come to my own conclusions through personal inquiry and investigation. I liked the independent aspect of the method I was learning.

Soon, I had the knowledge to access the nonphysical. I was learning how to direct my attention on making contact with my energetic family. I had found what I was looking for—a way to further my spiritual evolution. By arriving at my own perspectives, I learned to depend on myself as the means to acquire information from the nonphysical and foster my independence.

My mentor provided crucial feedback and support just as a

coach would. I was there to build a bridge, take excursions into the nonphysical, and open doors enabling existing relationships in other locations to come forward and find me.

Over time I began to understand the process was about reestablishing my inherent resources, including links and bonds already well-established in the nonphysical. Since these resources were already present, I was merely becoming reacquainted with existing connections. In so doing I could begin to experience the aspects of my essence, higher self, and energy system already participating in nonphysical environments. It became clear I was not alone. All people are inexorably connected to the nonphysical. This single observation would become a dominant theme in my life.

I was learning the skills of inner exploration without giving the process a name or label. During my life I had been influenced by many beliefs about spirituality. When I undertook nonphysical explorations, I thought I might learn something spiritual about myself. After a few months in the process, I got the impression the work I was doing was less about spirituality and more like homework. Through my studies I viewed the nonphysical as spiritual worlds. By connecting, I could begin to understand the far reach of my energetic system. I was changing and growing by becoming reacquainted with capabilities I already possessed.

The work I had undertaken was just so far outside the envelope of what I thought or imagined. To travel from here to nonphysical worlds was far more technical than spiritual. I was developing a pragmatic and efficient approach to building an internal workshop to test, confirm, or reject information I had learned since childhood about the physical world and beyond. I was especially attracted to the self-sufficient aspect of the work that cultivated my independence while developing my capabilities. As my mentor once said, "We don't become anything because we already are, yet we always create." It's what we are with instinctive awareness and the capability to join our energetic counterparts that enable our full creative potential.

I used to wonder if there was a phrase to represent this idea succinctly. My mentor used the term "spiritual evolution" to describe the inner journey. Yet even that label scarcely touches the experience of uniting with my higher self and energetic system.

One day I met my mentor at the office as usual. I told him I was grateful for everything he taught me. He had helped me acquire a solid understanding of self-exploration. I wasn't sure if I needed to continue making the weekly trips. He smiled and said, "You have what you came for. You don't need me any longer." At that moment I realized I wanted to continue the training. I still had more to learn. As I pulled back the layers of my energy system, my explorations raised many questions. At times I may have been compelled to ask my mentor his thoughts or push him for answers. Often, he would just smile and say I would have to find my own answers. I took his advice and focused on my energetic family and others in the nonphysical to answer my questions.

I was learning about the benefit of expanded perspectives to help me grasp a larger understanding not limited by my human self alone. The term "expanded perspectives" comes from the view of myself as an energy being in the physical environment, with its borders and limits, acquiring broader views from my energetic family and others in the nonphysical. By accessing my connections, I gained the benefit of a balanced view from both physical and nonphysical environments. I was also learning to extend my reach as broadly as my capabilities would permit, gaining a valuable understanding of the role other environments play in my life. Regarding the finer points of nonphysical architecture, an individual's energetic family is conceptually tricky because it does not necessarily follow the same relationships as an individual's physical family. An individual's energetic family are those physical or nonphysical beings that are part of the individual's higher self and, in some instances, nonphysical or physical beings that are or were linked to an individual over many physical existences, originating from the same system. One or more individuals, on Earth or other planets, can be linked to the same higher self, meaning the higher self can have one or many extensions into various areas of physicality. Each of these extensions is a physical individual. A larger number of related higher selves form a system and there are countless systems in the nonphysical. As I've said, an individual has existing associations with their energetic counterparts. Within the nonphysical are countless systems, and only a small minority focus on physicality. It is not uncommon for two or more individuals from the same system to be in physicality at the same time. But knowing about each other is extremely rare. An individual will have many associations with other individuals from different systems.

Thirty years ago, I undertook the journey of self-discovery with my mentor as a stepping stone to my higher self and system. This was a long and winding path to the fortune of my discoveries. I am grateful to be in a position to share this understanding. My lifetime of transcendental stories filled me with unique perspectives informed by my nonphysical experiences. I wrote this book for humanity. By sharing my journey, I hope to inspire others to become aware of their higher self and explore their potential.

TWENTY-ONE

Lion in the Tree Line: When the Higher Self Speaks

When we reach beyond ourselves, we inadvertently invite forward players from the Larger Field, and our system is there to keep an eye out for us. As I had begun to pay more attention along the journey, I had taken steps to align myself with my essence and learn to interface with nonphysical environments. The path I had undertaken became a bridge to broader experiences, and I was ready.

During this period, while living in Colorado I often took my German Shepherd, Buddha, for late-night hikes along a front range park near my home. I enjoyed our nighttime excursions when the air was still and the moon and stars cast their brightest glow on the fields and forest treetops. One night I found the familiar path that cut through tall prairie grass ascending the hillside and disappeared in a gulf of darkness at the tree line, where the boundary between what I could and could not see was a threshold to the unknown realms of the night. The excitement of late-night hikes flooded my senses with heightened awareness and sharpened my instincts. I loved the feeling of connection to the environment.

Buddha and I were to walk a mile through the thick forest, past 1,000-foot-tall flatiron boulders before emerging in the open fields on the other side of the park. As I moved steadily toward the tree line, a sudden sensation cut through my body and caused the hair to stand tall on my skin. I stopped in my tracks. A second later I heard a voice say to me, "Do not proceed. Return from where you came." My reaction was to acknowledge the voice as if responding to the urgency of a friend's warning beside me. I said, "Okay." Without hesitation I turned back. I asked myself, "What was that about?" This time the answer did not come as a voice, but as a warning of danger in my body, especially the sensation of tingling in my head and torso. I didn't doubt the danger for a moment. I followed the directions and continued down the path.

When I started on the path that night, I thought I was alone with my dog. That changed when I heard the voice. I sensed with every cell in my body I was not alone.

I started that evening with a casual walk to explore the physical world. Suddenly I was being pulled to understand the voice. But I recognized the voice. It had spoken softly in the back of my mind since my childhood. This time it was loud in my ear. I was being warned. Earlier that summer I heard the snarl of a mountain lion outside my back window one night. They occasionally came down from the backcountry and could be spotted slinking around town in the dark. An image entered my mind's eye. I saw a lion crouching in the tree line, stalking me. That was it, I was becoming aware of my system protecting me. I was learning that my nonphysical counterparts could directly communicate to me with images, a subtle voice in the back of the mind, or an outright audible voice spoken as if standing right next to me.

I began to look at myself operating in two locations simultaneously. I was caught between these two vastly different worlds that seemed to function relative to one another, as if joined by an unseen unifying force, and then there was me in the middle trying to figure out how I fit in. A stroke of insight, a gut feeling, and a voice comes along and shows me I'm already participating in both these worlds whether I know it, want it, or like it.

The message revealed stunning intelligence. The first part of the message come to me as a voice, warning me to turn back as I neared the tree line. Had I received the message of the lion stalking me, I may have reacted with fear and increased my danger. But the second part of the message came later when I was safe at home. I was struck by how the two parts of the message came when and where I needed to be informed.

To comprehend the other worlds at play, I aimed to plant

a foot in both the physical world and the world where the voice came from to establish a transdual moral stance, meaning focused on the physical and nonphysical environments, and acquire broader perspectives from the insights and experiences offered by both worlds. From this stance I would investigate what I perceived as my energetic system that seemed to operate beyond my present location in the Earth life system. I began to view myself as being split off from my higher self and energetic system, like a projection into the physical world.

I wanted to know more about my energetic family and how they could see what I could not see and provide real-time information or alerts, such as what I experienced on the trail that night. I was beginning to understand that the voice of my higher self was from the same location as insights, intuition, gut feelings, and hunches, having a beneficial and guiding quality in my life. Moreover, I understood I was never alone. My energetic core family has always been there. At times I might perceive their role in the background, but in reality, they are center stage in my life. As we become aware of our higher self, we discover our potential to put our lives in a far broader perspective, which helps us live with more resourcefulness.

TWENTY-TWO

Voice to Humanity: We Are All on the Path

One afternoon I lay down to meditate. As I relaxed deeply, a powerful message came to me, saying, "The next phase of humankind's evolution is its linking to the multiple in the Larger Field. All are concerned. There are no exceptions."

The message had complexities. It took me time to understand the broader implications of the message. My higher self eventually shed light on its meaning. The next phase of humankind's evolution is its linking to the multiple in the Larger Field. In this context, the "multiple" represents a human being's energetic core family, the multiple parts of ourselves forming an association of energies in nonphysical environments within the Larger Field. From there we acquire broader or expanded perspectives balanced between the physical and nonphysical as a unified, cohesive whole system.

What fascinated me about the message was its firm stance

that all people are involved in the next phase of humankind's evolution. There is much assistance from physical and nonphysical realms. After millennia, humankind is, at last, discovering existing relationships to reestablish linkage to the multiple. The emergence has already started—evolutionarily speaking, more people have started to operate in a linked fashion, tuning into their essence, building connections with their energetic counterparts, and the awareness of worlds beyond them, recognizing they play an important role in the larger unfolding of their spiritual evolution and that of humanity. The implications taking place planetarily are momentous. The pursuit of nonphysical connectivity begins with a desire to learn and grow with our essence and its existing links to our nonphysical counterparts. Other worlds are ours to experience. The steps to go from here to there starts with a thought, to set ourselves free of boundaries and grow to experience the Larger Field.

Years ago, a voice from my higher self offered me the guidance to reestablish existing connections in the nonphysical. What began with my lifetime of transcendental experiences evolved into investigating the source of intuition, insight, and beneficial voices which have played a fundamental role in humanity from the beginning of civilization.

Hearing supportive, guiding voices is nothing new for humans. Beneficial voices have been acknowledged by ancient civilizations throughout history, passing the knowledge of the nonphysical orally to future generations. Today there are tribal cultures around the globe guided by voices. To many in tribal communities, voices are considered normal. These societies operate on a principle of connection to spiritual worlds as a system to manage and adapt to the challenging physical environment. In Western societies, hearing beneficial voices is considered abnormal and not accepted by our culture. Connection to the nonphysical was once a natural occurrence among humans that has been forgotten. What is forgotten, however, can be remembered.

Each of our stories is the beginning of a far larger story. Wholeness is our birthright. Discovery is limitless. The more I experience the nonphysical, the more I realize how little I know. Our existence is mysterious. There are no ready-made answers. But questions keep us young, for they awaken insights and offer changing perspectives to learn and stretch our evolution. The one certainty for each of us is the very real potential to know ourselves, beginning with the awareness of our higher self. No one knows us better.

We cross the bridge to nonphysical worlds in the life process, between birth and departure to the energetic origin of humanity. As creators, we are predisposed to one purpose only—the application of our intention in the experiences of the Larger Field. You are an essence with a higher self and energetic family. Reject fear and anger to access the full accord of insight, intuition, and creativity, and unify the physical and nonphysical worlds. The discovery of wholeness expands your outlook, offering independence and freedom of spirit— the ultimate foundation of wealth—the only real wealth in the universe.

Always remember, we are energy beings first and foremost. The goal for each of us is to reach for our existing connections. Reach for other worlds beyond the street outside, the city around it, the sky above, the mountains, oceans, and deserts, to the furthest of multiple worlds in the Larger Field—and then come back.

Never forget you chose to be this actor, acting this specific part on that very stage called Earth. Always remember the Larger Field. For those on the path, it is the grand endless adventure. The ultimate voyage of your essence across the eons. The only journey that truly counts.

My final request as you experience your nonphysical journey:

Keep all this only as a possible. Keep your mind open and learn to discern.

From the Larger Field and me,

Stephen Daniel